FAITH, PSYCHOLOGY AND CHRISTIAN MATURITY

FAITH, PSYCHOLOGY AND CHRISTIAN MATURITY

MILLARD J. SALL

ZONDERVAN
PUBLISHING HOUSE   OF THE ZONDERVAN CORPORATION
GRAND RAPIDS, MICHIGAN 49506

I affectionately dedicate this book to
MARIE
who has been my faithful wife
and dedicated mother to our three sons —
Mark, Timothy, and Stephen.
Her loving care for our family permitted me more time
to spend on the contents of this book.
Her loving companionship through the years has given
me the zest for achievement without which
this work would have forever remained a fond dream.

Contents

Acknowledgments

I wish to acknowledge the following people for their sacrificial help: Jonny Hiskey and Shirley Schieber for help in the wording of the original manuscript; John Van Dixhorn, Dr. S. Philip Sutherland, Roger and Ann Stull, Dr. Vern Lewis, Dr. Paul Briggeman, Helen Kooiman, and Dr. Bernard Ramm for reading the manuscript critically and making helpful suggestions, constructive criticism, and new ideas to help strengthen the content of the book; Jo Ann Kraemer and Rowena Boehne for the typing and retyping of the various manuscripts; and the last of all, David J. Juroe for his helpful content suggestions and additions, the heavy burden of the work of correcting, editing, indexing, and arranging the various divisions of the book.

Introduction

FOR A LONG TIME, the church has heard this false inquiry: "Which will you look to — Christ or psychology — to meet your emotional needs?" The Christian has been made to feel that he must choose and that there is no meeting ground. Yet many a serious pastor, especially in recent years, has found that more and more of his time is taken up with counseling his parishioners concerning emotional and marital difficulties.

The sincere Christian asks, "Isn't Christ sufficient to meet man's emotional needs?" "Where is the work of the Holy Spirit in all these problems?" Many devout Christians feel guilty about their anxiety states, compulsions, depressions, and hostilities. They may spend years fighting these twisted and conflicting emotions either behind the belief that they are yet harboring some secret sin in their lives or that if they were only more yielded to Christ their problems would disappear.

Others, out of a sense of desperation, seek psychological help with the new fear that their faith may be destroyed or that all their convictions will crumble and they might yield to the sins of the flesh.

My purpose in writing this book is to attempt to harmonize the supposed conflict between these two — the emotional and the spiritual — and to point out that genuine psychological truth, when all dis- coveries are made, will not be in conflict with the Bible, the source of all divine truth.

This book is not an attempt to make an exhaustive study nor does its author claim to have all the answers to this most difficult subject. The purpose of this book is to stimulate the reader to a higher plane of spiritual and emotional understanding.

The book is a defense of the premise that psychological truth and evangelical Christianity can be harmonized. The goal of the book is to strengthen one's spiritual relationship with Christ through a deeper understanding of man's psychological nature.

The theological sections are in no way to be construed as an exhaustive exegetical study of the passages quoted. They are intended only to clarify the material presented in the book.

The book is not written for the general lay audience, nor is it written for the seasoned professional, but rather for the knowledgeable layman who is interested in the study of psychology and at the same time embraces the Christian faith as well as the pastors of Christian churches who every day are confronted with people and their problems. We see these ministers serving in a very key role in these days as therapists to offer as much help and support as possible to those who are burdened down with anxiety and who are unable to cope with the pressures of modern life.

All names used in the illustrations have been changed and any resemblances to known persons are coincidental.

PART I

What Psychology Teaches Us
About Ourselves

1

Know Thyself

Shall We Get Rid of Self?

IN A PERPLEXING world such as ours, many Christians are troubled about how they should feel about themselves. Some people feel the need of a good self-concept in order to survive the pressures and problems of a demanding and changing world. The housewife with the demands of children who are fighting all the time, the salesman who feels the pinch of reaching certain sales quotas, college students who realize the competitive crunch to attain — all must be able to function under stress.

Some feel caught in a trap between yielding all to Christ and maintaining a healthy self-concept, and so they live a life of conflict, operating with a double standard. On Sunday they lay all on the altar, but on Monday, in the busyness of the world, they are self-assertive in order to compete for a livelihood. They feel confused with the dilemma of how to sacrificially serve God and still survive in the complex, competitive, commercial world of the twentieth century. For example, a corporation vice president may yield to Christ in church on Sunday, but on Monday he may feel guilty when he leads the sales meeting, manages the production end of the business, and makes rapid decisions affecting profits because he finds himself unable to deal with it all. All of us experience this in some degree if we are fully honest with ourselves.

We Can't Escape Psychology

The battle seems to be narrowed down to the fields of psychological and biblical interpretation. Christians frequently say, "Well, psychology turns me off; the answers cannot lie there." It may turn them off, but they are still psychological beings. I know people who hate the word "psychology" but fail to realize that maybe 90 percent of their behavior originates from the unconscious and, as a result, influences more of what they are than they truly realize.

What kind of a person are you? What do you think of yourself? Are you a good person or a bad person? Psychology provides the tools to give one insight about these questions. Many people don't know how to look at themselves or realistically know how they feel about themselves. In order to evaluate yourself properly, it will be helpful to study the different world views about the self. There are numerous views and religions which teach that a person should try to get rid of "self" in order to have a fulfilled life.

A "Snuffed-out Candle"

Buddhists have some very interesting words to say about the "self." Buddha once said, "Existence and human suffering are frankly the same thing. And, since there are so many suffering human beings in the world, the thing we've got to do to get rid of suffering is to get rid of desire. You can step out of desire by sitting under a tree and meditating hours on end." That is what many of the Eastern religions teach. When you have meditated long enough you've entered a state called "Nirvana," or the state of the "snuffed-out candle." In other words, the way to get rid of your headache is to get rid of your head. That's what the Buddhist is really saying. Since existence and suffering are the same thing, step out of desire and you're not going to suffer anymore.

Impersonalize the Personal

The Hindu comes along and says, "What we've go to do to find true reality is to merge ourselves with the great world of energy, light, or something out there." In other words, make that which is too personal, impersonal. It is to have a kind of pantheistic view: Matter and God are one all-encompassing reality. If you're chopping up a weed in your backyard, you're chopping up an aspect of the entire world because the ground, creatures, people, and everything are one single reality. So then, the Buddhists say, "Get rid of desire which is a manifestation of self," and the Hindu says, "Take something that's personal and make it totally impersonal."

But let me ask you, is that really going to work? The fingerprints on your hand prove that you are a unique individual. Each individual has fingerprints that no one else has, proving that every individual has differences and that he is unique.

Even the longing of the human heart is for somebody to remember "*my* name." And to remember "*my* birthday." Now be honest, don't you have need for some personal attention? You may not want to ask for it too loudly or directly, but you surely like it when you get it. Somebody once said, "I get sick and tired of getting Christmas cards;

most of the people never write any news in them." I may have felt that way at one time, but a plain old Christmas card with my name on it means so much, especially when the sender went to school with me. There is something about that personal interest that we like.

You cannot eradicate the self; it is impossible. To attempt to change a person so that he has no feelings at all is completely unrealistic. To be part of the great One, as the Hindus believe, may work for some, but for the Christian the worth of the individual soul is the emphasis.

Getting to Know Yourself

The third way to look at yourself is through the eyes of psychology. It has merit but will fall short of its goal to help people find true selfhood when it denies the spiritual end of man.

Modern secular psychology says, "If you know yourself, you will be a better-adjusted person." This started with philosophers even before Socrates. Then he came along and said, "Know thyself."

Psychologists today are very much interested in having people know themselves, too. A child walks into a counselor's office and is asked, "What is your name?" He may know that. "Where are you going in life?" "I don't know." "What do you want to be?" "Well, I'm not sure." "Who are you?" "I don't know." Many people are like that. They are similar to machines. They do things and don't know why. They don't understand their feelings. The modern secular psychologist, as well as the Christian psychologist, says, "We must help that person come to know himself."

This is why I like my work. I see approximately forty-five people a week in the office. People say, "How do you do it?" It's not difficult when you love it. Why do I love it? Because I find meaning in life through what I am doing. Countless people don't know themselves or are in conflict about themselves. My job is to help them discover themselves.

Modern secular psychology is really saying, "If you come to know yourself, you will do it by coming to know somebody else." In other words, nobody comes to know himself through his own eyes. He can know himself only as he is known through a real encounter with some other person.

For instance, when my youngest son was three years of age, he came up and threw his arms around my legs, smiled and looked up into my face and said, "Daddy, am I a good boy or a bad boy?" That may seem funny, but he didn't really know. If I were to say, "You're a spoiled little brat," he would actually have believed that he was a bad boy. If I said he was a good boy, he would believe he was a good boy. The basic concept that you and I get about ourselves comes from other people, especially our parents.

Since we can never eradicate ourselves or become impersonal beings through some kind of self-denial, it is all-important to discover who we are and what we are through other kinds of efforts. Because it takes others to truly enable a person to come to know himself, this book is written to promote that discovery. This can be done by an understanding of the term "ego" in both the biblical and psychological contexts. Through the blending and integration of the two fields, a person will find a higher meaning and a more wholesome, balanced life and a better understanding of himself than he ever thought possible.

2

What Is the Ego?

What Distinguishes One Person From Another?

PERSONAL IDENTITY IS best understood by examining the meaning of the word "ego" found in the Greek New Testament. It is translated "I." The "I," then, is my identity, which differentiates me from other people and/or things. It is the line of demarcation between what is "I" and what is not "I." When Bobby is born, for example, he does not know he is Bobby. Initially, he feels that he is the whole world; nothing else exists. However, when he feels hunger pangs, he can't feed himself. His mother must feed him. Soon he discovers that he is separate from her, but that she is indispensable to him because she fulfills his physical needs.

As Bobby grows, he learns to distinguish between himself, other people, and objects. When he plays with his fingers or toes, he discovers they are part of him. When he plays with a toy or book, he discovers they are not a part of him but separate from him. This early understanding is referred to by psychologists as the formation of the "body-ego." Bobby also learns to distinguish between mother's voice and his own vocal sounds. Gradually, different aspects of mother are put together. The image of her that he sees is integrated with her sounds. He discovers that sight, sound, smell, and touch are all different aspects of the same person whom he will soon identify as mother. He is now developing an ego. He and mother and other things are separate. He is perceiving what is "I" and what is not "I." This is how we learn that we have an ego.

The ego is self-awareness. It is what distinguishes "I" from what is not "I" throughout an individual's life. It functions like a giant radar system, constantly measuring inner impulses and drives, such as hunger, thirst, and fatigue, while at the same time perceiving stimuli from reality outside the body, such as sight, sound, feel, and touch. It also reconciles the demands arising from within the body and the demands outside the body.

As this self-structure emerges, it becomes the essential integrating core of one's personality — the reference point around which the person's experience and reaction patterns are organized. When a problem arises, it is perceived, thought about, and acted upon in relation to the self.

Fundamental to the individual's self-awareness are the assumptions he develops about himself and the world. These assumptions are of three kinds:

1. *reality assumptions* — his view of things as he thinks they really are, the kind of person he is, and the nature of the world he lives in;
2. *value assumptions* — his view of the way things should be, of right and wrong, good and bad, desirable and undesirable;
3. *possibility assumptions* — his concept of how things could be, of possibilities for change, and of opportunities for personal growth and social progress.

So a healthy ego is an absolute necessity if one is to have a balanced and healthy perspective of life.

Christianity Does Not Reject the Ego

With this description of ego in mind, it would hardly seem that dedicated Christian living would mean rejecting the ego or self. There could be no spiritual life without an ego, for there would be no sanity, no reality, no personality to relate to one's fellowman or to God. Many Christians feel that egotism, pride, boasting, and making personal claims far beyond one's ability are evidences of too much ego.

We must, however, be careful to differentiate between a healthy ego and egotism. Since the job of a healthy ego is to appraise reality objectively, the person who makes grandiose claims out of proportion to his abilities has a weak ego because he is not testing reality accurately. His boasting is a fantasy he has constructed to compensate for feelings of failure and weakness.

For example, a speaker who frequently reminds his audience that he does not have stage fright and that he is at ease in front of an audience is really trying to assure himself that he is not frightened. The little boy who threatens the bully by saying, "My dad can beat up your dad," is actually seeking to compensate for his feelings of inadequacy. The singer who has a beautiful voice, but tells people she really can't sing, is searching for praise. She is guilty of pride. She may be afraid that she may make a mistake and is therefore afraid of other people's scorn.

The Lord gave talents to all of us and expects us to increase them to glorify Him. If we have put down our ego so that we are either unaware of our talents or afraid to use them, we are not very effective Christians. A good, healthy ego increases our ability to do the Lord's work by making us aware that we are unique creatures with God-given talents to be used for the betterment of mankind. A Christian with a weak ego simply doesn't have the faith in himself to challenge others with the demands of real Christian growth.

Personal Faith Enhances the Ego

Many non-Christians appear to have strong egos. A man who does not know Christ may have good relationships with other people. Outwardly, he may appear stable, happy, and fulfilled — able to communicate with people and understand them. If he is a devoted humanist, he may participate in many philanthropic endeavors. He may be active in the Red Cross, the United Fund, or various service organizations. He may have a devoted family and a successful business. Yet at times he feels there is something missing in his life. His ego is not complete, since he has not as yet accepted or discovered the ultimate reality found in Christ. He spends his life looking. He may start collecting art treasures or travel to distant lands. He is restless and may not really be at peace with himself. He is like the ballerina dancer, who, when asked if her fame had not given her much pleasure, said, "It is a strange thing, but after many curtain calls, much applause, and tremendous acclaim, I go to my room. There, when alone, I feel a desert in my heart."

The ego, then, can best be described as the *executive branch* of the mind which makes decisions. The ego perceives, tests, and selects or rejects data and behavior patterns. An underdeveloped ego is incapable of evaluating reality and making proper decisions as they relate to the situation or problem confronting the individual. The development of the ego is a natural pattern of growth and maturity. It is the self-awareness of the individual that differentiates him from other people. Since no two creatures are alike, it is essential that each person recognize who he is, how he relates to other people, why he reacts the way he does, and what factors have contributed to the development of his personality.

The final end of man is spiritual. The mysteries and complexities of life must have purpose and meaning, or man is simply a biological freak. Peace of mind, power to overcome problems, and faith in the future are free gifts of the abounding grace of God. God created man with an ego, which man must not suppress or crush. To deny one's ego, then, is to deny the handiwork of God.

3

The Self — Its Various Parts

The Mind May Be Observed by the
Actions and Conflicts of a Person

To BETTER KNOW ourselves and the way we come to understand our behavior, it is necessary for us to consider the parts of the mind.

Psychoanalysis teaches that every person's mind consists of three divisions. These divisions are called "hypothetical constructs" because they cannot be located in the body. They can be inferred only in the conflicts, actions, and motivations of a person. It is important to recognize that these three divisions, which were first set forth by Sigmund Freud, are only pegs that help us to better understand the area of behavior. They are in no way to be considered final and authoritative. A critical look at Freud will be discussed later (chapter 13), since he is a controversial figure among evangelical Christians.

The first division is called the "id." The id represents the impulses that arise within the body. It consists of what we might call the basic physical drives. It produces a mental representation of a bodily need, such as hunger, thirst, or sex. When hunger tension arises in the stomach, we may see a mental image of food. The more tired we become, the more our thoughts center on soft beds or places of comfort. Sexual tension arising in the body produces a desire for a sex partner. A person may be bewildered by what it is that makes him think or do these things. The urge within is what analysts identify as the id. This is described by a woman who came to me a few years ago.

> She had been diagnosed as a schizophrenic of long standing and had been reared in a Christian home. She was in her early forties and loved the Lord with all her heart. She attended prayer meeting and all the other general services of the church. Her problem was that she had an unusually strong sex drive. As with most schizophrenics, control of these impulses was impossible for her. Whenever the drive became too strong, she

found herself sexually involved with a variety of different men and sometimes quite indiscriminately. Afterward, she punished herself to atone for her behavior but the feeling of guilt about her sin only created more anxiety and even less control. She once said to me, "I feel like I am an egoless blob. I don't even have enough power to organize my thinking to concentrate on reading the Bible. Even my praying is very erratic."

This is a perfect illustration of the function of the id without ego control.

Not long ago a man came to my office feeling that he was going to kill somebody. He had prayed about it and asked God to take away his terrible angry feelings, but nothing seemed to work. He said that sometimes he was overwhelmed with these feelings and would start throwing furniture around the house, knock his wife on the floor, and start beating on her. The children would become frightened and cry and scream. This made him more enraged and he would swear at them. He said to me, "I just can't get any control of myself. What can I do?"

Observation shows that id impulses operate in every human being. They are a *normal* part of everyone's make-up and they are concerned with seeking and experiencing pleasure and avoiding pain. They are abnormal, as shown in the illustrations above, when there is lack of ego control to channel them in the proper direction.

These id impulses are also characterized by immediacy: "I want it and I want it now." The id by itself is totally unteachable. It is incapable of learning, has no value system, and is incapable of profiting from any past experience. The id, then, represents desires and needs arising within the body.

The Place of Conscience

On the other side of the personality structure from the id is the "superego." It is an external pressure for conformity to a set of standards placed upon the human ego. It is "super" because it is "over," thus bigger and more powerful than the ego. People know it as the "conscience." Since the young child needs love, especially parental love, he learns to conform to his parents' standards. To obey brings acceptance and love; to disobey brings disapproval or punishment. Therefore, the child internalizes the parents' "dos and don'ts" in order to obtain their approval, affection, and acceptance. In other words, the parental demands, which are external, are taken inside. This means that things learned from other people, mainly the parents, become integrated as a part of one's own self.

In order to keep the parent "omnipotent," which the child needs to do, he creates ideals about what the perfect parent should be, especially when he sees any faults in his parents. This is called "fantasy," which is a way of escaping reality. Infatuation is the result of a young person's discovery of another young person who coincides with his idealized image of the perfect parent of the other sex. You can't talk him out of this infatuation, for "love is blind"; it is blinded by the idealized fantasy.

As the child grows older, social values influence his superego. For example, mode of dress, acceptable language, or civil law lay down certain ground rules for the individual's acceptance by society. The superego is greatly affected by one's religious faith; the commandments, precepts, and rules of his particular faith become his standards.

The power of the superego may be seen by the following illustration. Though the man's behavior was influenced by social values, it was distorted by an overactive superego.

> A man once came to my office, saying he felt that he had committed the unpardonable sin, that he had never done anything right, and that God should strike him dead. He felt guilty for expressing his opinions to anyone because he should consider other people and not himself. He had compulsions to stop in at every police station to find out if he had caused an accident. One night on television when it was announced that the police were looking for a hit-and-run driver, he called the police department and confessed the crime. Of course, he had never even been in the city where the accident had occurred. He said he felt a great sense of relief by confessing.
>
> But the guilt never went away. The next day he visited a number of different ministers. Many of them prayed with him and he felt temporarily relieved, only to find he needed to repeat the process again and again. He knew he was a Christian but this never seemed to help him get over the cruel and severe memories of how his mother always told him he was such a bad boy. He even found himself making serious mistakes at his job so that he would be punished. His need for relief was overwhelming.
>
> One time his wife accidentally had brought home a neighbor's book in a bag when she was visiting in the neighbor's home. He felt so guilty about it that he could not sleep, feeling that this was stealing. His compulsion drove him to the neighbor's house in the middle of the night to return the book and to confess his wife's "theft."

Analysis shows that one's superego may be healthy, corrupt, or unrealistic, depending upon which stimuli influenced him the most and whether they were healthy, corrupt, or unrealistic. For example, a harsh, overdemanding parent could create in the child a harsh, rigid way of looking at life.

Who Am I?

The third and most central part of the human mind is the ego itself. The ego stands between the id and the superego and attempts to resolve any conflicts between them. As noted in the preceding chapter, it reconciles the demands arising from within and outside the body. The value systems must be internalized. Conflicts arise when these components of the personality are out of balance. If the hunger drive from the id signals the ego to eat a steak and the ego complies, then the id drives subside. But if the person's religious training signals that it is a sin to eat meat, then, if the steak has been eaten, the ego will be punished by feeling a sense of guilt.

If the id says, "I want a chocolate candy bar," but the superego says, "Don't eat that! You're too fat," the ego is caught in conflict. Should the ego yield to the id or to the superego? A healthy ego might resolve the conflict by buying a dietetic candy bar. Or, as another example, the id might say, "I want a Cadillac." The superego responds, "You don't have the money, and if you steal it, you will be put in jail." Once again the ego is caught in conflict, but this time it might solve the dilemma by compromising with the purchase of a Volkswagen. If the conflict is too severe, it might cause enough anxiety to be converted into a depression, obsessive behavior, compulsive acts, phobias, sociopathic character structures, or even psychoses — all of which we will deal with later. These reactions are actually escape mechanisms which the ego uses to defend itself against anxiety.

Freud Oversimplified

In recent years much criticism has been leveled at Sigmund Freud because he explained human behavior in too mechanical a way. This criticism is valid and he himself recognized later in life the value of man's relationships with people through a strong and healthy ego.

The current ego psychologists — such as Schafer, Jacobson, Hartmann, Fairbairn, Erikson, Winnicott, and others—started where Freud left off. They view man as more than an ego system that is somewhat like a computer. They describe man as a person with a warmth and personality, which they call "the self." To effect a cure in emotionally disturbed people, they say, it takes more than the mere cognitive knowledge of simply recognizing a block in one of the psychic or sexual stages of development in early childhood. Current thinkers rightly want us to go beyond that by seeing man with the ability to relate with full warmth toward another human being. They tell us that the important key to the personality, rather than being a physiological or biological bias, is the object relationship with other people.

For example, current thinkers would say that a woman who has a "daddy hang-up" from the past is also frightened in her present existence and it is her present fears that ought to be dealt with as much as the resolution of the earlier problem. In the treatment of her fears, they play down Freud's Oedipus complex and give it a less important part in the resolution of neurosis. Although the complex is there and in certain cases must be dealt with, real treatment of a past conflict usually demands dealing with a much earlier period of life and the discovery of a deep, unsatisfied oral need denied by the person, who withdraws into a world of his own. He lives as a detached, shut-in personality with a hopelessly frightened infantile ego that gave up real relationships with people as unattainable. This kind of person seeks safety in regression to the earliest time of life where there was warmth and safety.

It has been our experience that the core of most deeply ingrained neuroses comes before the Oedipal period and that real healing involves the person's allowing himself to let his guard down and so making it possible for another human being to reach the frightened, detached little child in him that has been so closely guarded.

We Can Learn From Freud

In conclusion, it must be stated that Freud's view of man is incomplete because he fails to see man as a total person. His view, however, has opened many avenues toward understanding neuroses and this should not be discounted. We can learn from Freud as well as anyone else. The lesson for us is that we must not be locked into any one man or system as infallible for this inhibits growth or knowledge. We need continual study and research by all sincere students of human behavior.

Let us evaluate and compare this psychoanalytic material with Scripture. The Bible teaches that "the heart is deceitful above all things, and desperately corrupt" (Jeremiah 17:9). The "heart" in this context corresponds to what the Bible describes as the "old self" (Romans 6:6) or what the theologian calls the "old nature," which men inherited from Adam and which is very similar to what the psychologist terms the "uncontrollable id impulses."

Carl Jung, a world-famous psychoanalyst and author who eventually broke with Sigmund Freud, developed a personality theory that has similarities to the scriptural teachings of Adam's fall. According to Jung, in addition to the personal unconscious — consisting of the individual's experiences that once were conscious but have been forgotten, suppressed, or repressed — the individual also has a collective unconscious, consisting of "racial" memories established through the thousands of years of man's existence and inherited in the brain structure in the form of "primordial images" or "archetypes." An archetype is an inherited universal image or idea that contains a large element of emotion and is elicited by some aspect of the individual's life situation. Thus the archetype of "mother," the image of the mother figure, is elicited by the child's own mother. How well Jung's theory coincides with Psalm 51:5 — "In sin did my mother conceive me." At the time of the fall of man, the normal id drives — thirst, hunger, and sex — were all present. After the fall, these normal needs became exaggerated and inflamed. Man lost his regard for others and became an enemy of God. He broke God's laws. These exaggerated, unteachable, valueless, uncontrolled, pleasure-seeking impulses correspond with what the Bible calls sin. Thus David's lament could be classed as a cry of grief because of his inherited sinful nature.

Paul describes the conflict arising from these impulses-gone-awry: "I do not know what I am doing. For what I want to do I do not do, but what I hate I do. . . . I know that nothing good lives in me, that is, in my sinful nature. For I have the desire to do what is good, but I cannot carry it out. . . . What a wretched man I am! Who will rescue me from this body of death?" (Romans 7:15, 18, 24). Paul conceded that his ego at times was overwhelmed by these id impulses, but the saving grace of God through Christ helped him to overcome sin.

Conversion changes man's desires, but it doesn't rid him of temptation. The tempted ego receives a boost from God, who functions like a great Superego, so the person will not yield to temptation. God never intended that man should have to combat sin alone. This is one result of the death and resurrection of Christ for lost men. God came to earth to experience, as man, the human condition. Christ felt fatigue, thirst, and hunger so that He could experience human wants. Thus, the acceptance of Christ breaks down the wall of isolation from God and fellowman and restores man's relationship to God, helping him to cope with the problems of his existence. The Lord does for His child what the good parent does for his child who is not yet strong enough to face the conflicts and challenges of life.

The Role of Faith

In order to understand the phenomenon of life, we must admit that there is great divergence in heredity and environment. Some people have experienced relatively happy childhoods. Others have been frustrated by split loyalties, as in the case of divorce, or by parental rejection and/or indifference. The following illustration in a marked way points up the results of rejection by parents. Emotional damage can be created in their children.

"We were always treated as though we were never there, and I don't feel I even know who I am. Do you know who I am?

If you do, please tell me." These somber words were once spoken to me by a very disturbed patient — a mother of four children. She went on to say that her father was a very cold, hard-working businessman. He was seldom home. When he was, he was lost in the newspaper or the television.

She remembered as a child that her father never interacted with the family at all. She felt she could never talk to him. When she tried to get his attention by saying, "Daddy, watch me skip my rope," he either did not hear her or would just look up with a disgusting grin, as much as to say, "Why are you bothering me?"

Her relationship with her mother was not much better. Her mother was always out socializing. When she brought people into her nice home she would show them all the lovely antiques she had collected from Greece, Italy, and France. Once in a while, she remembered, if she was in her room when they were walking by, her mother said to the touring party, "Oh, incidentally, this is my daughter Nancy." She said that acceptance and understanding were missing in the home. There was never any feedback of emotion. She began to feel rejection more and more as she was left with babysitters. She came to feel that she really didn't exist. Now as a grown woman in the counseling chamber, she was asking, "Do I really exist? Am I real?"

She admitted that she had absolutely no confidence in any of her decisions and felt terribly hungry for some kind of interaction with people in order to find out who she was and if she was a real person.

The cold, rejecting parent oftentimes stunts the human identity of the child. Human emotional growth and character development then become distorted or arrested.

Reactions to emotionally damaging parents trigger reactions in the child's relationship with other people, and in fact, his world. He believes everyone will treat him as his parents did. If he felt unloved at home, he is very likely to feel that no one loves him. He will be beset by insecurity, fear, and guilt that are not consistent with the real situation. Because of his fear of parental rejection for certain acts, he may go back to an earlier stage of development where he felt safe. In essence, he remains a child emotionally.

We have all heard the expression, "Touch an adult and you find a child." Paul stated that when he became an adult, he put away childish things (1 Corinthians 13:11). This may be true for the apostle Paul, but it is not necessarily true of all Christians. It is one thing to be saved by Christ, but it is quite another thing to be a mature Christian. Salvation is not instantaneous growth. It means a new growing relationship with Christ which was broken by the fall of man. In Adam we all die. In Christ, we are all made alive because we have a new relationship with God. Through the ministry of the

Holy Spirit the person may gain a new motivation and value system to help control his id impulses. He has discovered a new purpose in life, one that gives him justification for his present existence, a meaning to his daily life, and a positive goal to work toward.

Beyond Ourselves

It is important to realize that Christ saves the person *where he is in life*. The saved man still has the same name, the same face, the same physique, and the same personality that he had before. Salvation is not a cure-all for all of life's problems, including present physical stress or emotional immaturity. Salvation is "of the soul"; a spiritual experience that enables man to relate to God now and throughout eternity. The Scripture admonishes us first to "grow in grace and knowledge of our Lord and Savior Jesus Christ" (2 Peter 3:18) then to work out our own salvation.

To give practical meaning to this admonition, try to imagine that life is a train trip from Los Angeles to Chicago. Some people never leave Los Angeles. Some stop in Denver because they are frightened to go on. Some get to Chicago, but the city (situation) brings forth unpleasant memories, so they go back to Denver and stop there. If we stop growing emotionally at a certain point in life, this is called "fixation." If we retreat, this is called "regression." Personality development is like the train trip, and the analyst seeks to find out why the person is afraid to proceed. God saves man "where he is" and puts him on the train toward the abundant Christian life, but He doesn't coerce him to go all the way. Man has choices about where he will stop. The man who stops short of God's expectation for him may well have a personality problem.

Since learning reasonable reactions and responses to the struggle of life begins with our parents, it is easy to understand how the child who is neglected in parental guidance will be left in a vacuum, unable to face the mysteries of life.

When I was in one of my pastorates, a young, fine-looking woman in her early twenties came to hear me preach for several Sundays. She seemed to listen intently and showed all the signs of conviction of sin as the sermon was preached. After she came for six Sundays, she phoned me at the study and said she would like to see me. She said she was a dental hygienist.

"I have been listening to your sermons for a number of weeks now," she said, "and I feel that I would really like to accept Christ as you have been preaching from the Bible. But there is something blocking me. I don't know what it is."

I thought there might be some deep sin she didn't want to give up or that it might be strictly a case of satanic oppression. So before speaking to her, I just kept on listening to her story.

She said, "I just can't seem to submit to God as my heavenly Father and I also resent the Lord's Prayer intensely." With these words she began to show signs of being visibly shaken and fearful. I said to her, "I'd like for you to tell me more about your relationship with people." In reply she said, "They are not good, especially toward me. That is the reason I have never married. I just can't imagine living with a man. The idea of it sounds like a living hell."

It was then that I became intensely interested in hearing about her relationship with her father. She said he was a very cruel man. "I was reared in a small coal mining town in West Virginia. He was so angry all the time. He was also an alcoholic and I can remember him beating my mother and sister. I was deathly fearful of him. I felt if I didn't say or do exactly the right thing, he would beat me, and on some occasions he did just that." I then said to her, "How could you then pray, 'Our Father who art in heaven,' without seeing a terrible, unrealistic punishing God, rather than a tender, loving heavenly Father who unconditionally accepts you and desires your fellowship?"

In the following weeks, as we talked together, she became acutely aware of her fears about God as a punishing and mean person, out to destroy her. Through our conversations she also became aware that not all men were like her father. As we got deeper and deeper into her childhood experiences she began to realize that these fears, which were very real then, did not have to be carried over into every present situation now. She suddenly said one day, "I have just discovered that not all men are like my father. You are a man and you listen to me; you understand; you do not judge me or lash back or punish me."

From that point on, she felt a sense of tremendous relief and could even begin to accept herself and the angry feelings about her father. It was also at this point that her attitude toward God as her heavenly Father completely changed. She received a new image of God as a loving Father who was kind, generous in mercy, and genuinely concerned about her. She did accept Christ, was baptized, and joined the local fellowship. She is still active in her church and is serving on one of the church boards.

This story clearly demonstrates how a person's relationship with his parents may actually determine his view of God. Only by relating to another person in a healthy, understanding way, will most people find a deep and personal relationship with God.

An atheist may be a person who has had a bad relationship with his father — or possibly he has had no father to relate to at all. Since God is called "Father" and since this person can't be angry with his father in reality, he handles his hostility by projecting it onto God. Thus, the atheist is antagonistic toward God but often doesn't understand why.

The more we understand the three parts of the mind, their relationship to each other, and their interaction on our actions and beliefs, the more we will be capable of growing in Christian concern and compassion. The Christian life should be a constant growth toward maturity, but a personality hang-up may stunt that growth, causing the Christian to doubt, and this in turn may cause anxiety, depression, fear, and guilt. We will enlarge upon the concept of psychological maturity in the following chapter.

4

The Stages in Normal
Ego Development

Maturity Is a By-Product of Emotional Growth

PSYCHOLOGICALLY, THE FIRST requisite for personal maturity is the development of the ability to see ourselves and the world around us as objectively as possible and to face the realities of life. *Spiritually,* man responds as a unique individual to God and becomes bound by the sovereign, divine will. Christian growth is measured by man's increasing awareness of the power of the Spirit that works inside him and by his increasing triumph over temptation. It is a progressive process toward perfection.

Reality is often unpleasant and anxiety may undermine our constant efforts to feel good about ourselves. Unless we accept ourselves as good people once we have received the Lord, we can hardly serve as witnesses for Christ. Some people think spiritual maturity is only the result of persistence in Bible reading, prayer, church attendance, and abstinence from worldly practices. The mature Christian practices these things to enhance his life, but he also participates in an active, dynamic interaction in this world.

Who Is a Mature Person?

In this chapter we are concerned with what is psychological maturity, where and how it can be stunted, and in what way immaturity can actually inhibit our spiritual growth and development.

Many descriptions have been made about the mature personality by various writers. Some examples follow: The mature person is free from disabling conflicts within his personality. He is at peace with himself. He accepts himself, other people, and his faith. He recognizes his own faults, evaluates them, and tries realistically to change them. He is centered upon the problems he must face in reality rather than the constant problems within himself. He is not overly dependent upon other people; neither is he detached, totally independent, or aloof.

The mature person has the ability and the desire to share his love, ideas, money, time, and himself. He is able to delay his immediate impulses for something better and more lasting. He is able to accept love and to give love. He feels comfortable with people and enjoys interacting with them, yet at times he enjoys solitude and privacy. He takes time to meditate, reevaluate himself, and reexamine his goals in life. He takes problems and stresses in stride, accepting the fact that they must be met and dealt with. He does not panic or go to pieces but works the problem or frustration through, and he grows in experience as he does so. His life has a consistency about it.

Maturity shows in all areas of his life: church, home, school, work, and recreation. Such an individual has a special appreciation for the simple things of life — a smile, a flower, the wonders of nature. He finds meaning and purpose in his day-to-day activities and is not caught up in the rat race of the acquisition of wealth for wealth's sake nor wasting his time on the treadmill of trying to improve his social position. He is not chasing mirages of fame, fortune, and flattery. The commonplace comforts of life, such as marriage, children, friends, satisfaction of a job well done, and stimulating recreation hold meaning for him. He is not driven by unattainable wants, whose elusiveness frustrates him. He is self-motivated and in control of his thoughts, words, and deeds. He can think deeply about the evasive mysteries of life and at times can lose himself in the mystical aspects of the universe, but he never loses a sense of his own identity.

He possesses a consistent, moral character-structure. He is not easily led by the crowd or cultural irregularities nor is he susceptible to propaganda or brainwashing. Yet he is not rigid. For instance, he is able to accept change, respond to new challenges, and regard different viewpoints in people with tolerance.

The mature person, then, is able to adapt and adjust to his world. He sees himself and his world objectively, realizing that it takes great courage and resolution at times to live in this world as a responsible, aware adult. He has developed a self-sustaining relationship with other people that is a fine balance between dependency and independency. He is willing to face reality and give up the world of childhood with its fantasies and rationalizations.

Since character-structure and personality are formed in the early years of life, psychologists feel that fixations and regressions to early childhood are important to know about. A fixation occurs when the child reaches such a traumatic point that emotional development or maturity stops there and advances no further. Regression occurs when the child reverts back after having advanced to a given point. These defense mechanisms actually become "blocks" that prevent growth and maturity. There is agreement among most psychologists that the most comfortable, secure, and carefree stage of life is that of the embryo in the womb. There is automatic nourishment and elimination, perfect temperature control, and safety from accident or injury. When a person who faces a tough life situation crawls into bed, pulls up the covers, and curls into a ball, he is subconsciously regressing to that secure state of contentment he had in his mother's womb.

> This was beautifully illustrated one afternoon when Marlene came for her regular appointment. She appeared very weak and frightened. As she talked, she became worse. The more she talked, the more it became evident that she just could not cope with her anxiety. Suddenly she drew up her legs and froze in that state. She had regressed back into the perfect fetal position.

Marlene found that her anxiety at that moment was too great and she felt much more secure and safe in that comforting position.

Totally Dependent

Watching a baby grow is a key in understanding how people normally mature on an emotional level. The stages of development are quite clear. When a baby is born, his life is dependent upon his mother. He is in what psychologists identify as the *passive-dependent* position.

His whole life revolves around his mouth at this stage. Everything — his bottle, fingers, and blanket — he puts into his mouth. He is totally helpless without his mother. If she is absent too much of the time or is so anxious and tense that she seems rigid and rejecting, then the baby is unable to relate to her. It's quite possible that he may never develop an adequate ego, because of this lack of identification. If he stops at this point in his development, he may develop severe emotional problems in later life. He will drift off into a fantasy world of his own and never be able to relate to the real world.

Food and Love Equated

A baby moves from the oral-passive position to the *oral-aggressive* position. Life still revolves around the mouth, but the baby becomes more aggressive. Teething causes him to bite the nipple off the bottle, chew on toys, and even bite mother's fingers at times. During this stage of life, the baby equates food with love. When he is fed, he is held by his mother. He experiences the warmth of her body as she cuddles him and talks to him. He senses her love. If a baby's love needs are not met, if his mother props a bottle in a holder for him instead of holding him, if she is too busy to hold him and fondle him, then his love needs are not properly met. This kind of indifference on the part of the mother may result in a baby's developing into a "love addict" in adult life. He will seek the love of other people, but at the same time be anxious about their response for fear of being rejected again. Of course, although this is in the subconscious level, it is very real. Such a person will be more prone to deep, depressive spells. He will never think enough of himself to develop a good strong ego, because his first love object, his mother, didn't seem to like him.

An analogy can be made to the building of a wall. If there is a small crack in the wall at its foundation, the rest of the bricks might cover this up, but when the same situation arises that caused that original crack, the stress will be too much and the crack will widen and the foundation will weaken.

For example, suppose that a baby feels rejection because his mother never talked to him. He might develop quite normally. But if he marries a person who also is silent and undemonstrative, he will begin to feel the rejection he felt in early childhood. He may regress to that early stage and experience tremendous anxiety about his self-worth. This anxiety may manifest itself in overeating, which is an oral act that subconsciously makes him feel loved, or he may start drinking heavily and develop into an alcoholic.

Many Christians who have a problem in this area of development may have a desire to start smoking, which is another oral gratification, and find the habit almost impossible to break. If they stop smoking, they may start eating to excess. Their unconscious still equates food with love, and the feeling is that a sense of love will come with eating, drinking, or smoking — all of which are experiences relating to the mouth. This kind of need is depicted in the following story.

Betty once heard me in a Christian Family Living Seminar at a local church. After one of the sessions, she said, "I have been wanting to talk to someone for years about my problem." We made an appointment and she told me her story.

"I have always been a nervous, high-strung person. I am eighteen years old and am a Christian and I want to follow the Lord with all my heart. But when I get up-tight I invariably reach for a cigarette and am now smoking up to three packs a day. I know this is bad for my health and I want to quit in the worst way.

"A while back I went to a smoking clinic and quit cold but then something even worse happened. I began to be a compulsive eater. I was always in the refrigerator looking for something, emptying the candy dish, or opening a bottle of soda pop. This put on pounds rapidly. You know, Doctor, it seems that unless I have something in my mouth all the time I feel terribly insecure. So I decided it is better to smoke than to put on all those pounds. I really don't like either way, though.

"When I was in high school I even experimented with drugs. When I suddenly recognized what I was doing, I realized this was a course that would lead to disaster. I also have the need to see my doctor constantly to relieve my aches and pains. My medicine cabinet looks like a pharmacy and it seems I am always swallowing a pill.

"I also have an insatiable need for love and feel like a little girl who would like to be held by a motherly type of person. It just seems like I need bodily warmth and touch all the time. I also have never told anyone this before but I have a baby bottle that I suck at bedtime filled with milk."

In the following months, it became evident to Betty that she had regressed to a stage of early development. She began to see, with the help of therapy, that she just wanted to remain a little girl and was dodging the maturer realities of adulthood by such behavior. She had to see that in order to be a mature adult and to realize her full potentialities, she had to surrender these mother needs. As the insights began to dawn, she became more aggressive, less demanding. She began to take responsibility for her own behavior and saw the futility of depending on oral crutches. One day she said, "I realize I am now an adult and mother is never going to come and it wouldn't be the same now anyway." Although these things are still intermittently a problem, she is slowly growing to such an extent that she is gaining control over them and making a contribution to society by helping others.

The need for oral satisfaction is now believed to be one cause of stomach ulcers. The gastric juices keep secreting in an attempt to digest food, the symbol of early love. When food is not eaten, the digestive juices damage the lining of the stomach. People who have ulcers have great dependency needs, although they may appear to be very independent, secure, and serene.

Independence

As a baby grows beyond the stage when all experience relates to the mouth, he soon develops his own independence. He discovers he can say no to his mother.

In other words, he can rebel as an independent entity, separate from his mother. He begins to make demands, because he realizes that he is no longer totally dependent upon her. This independent action takes place during the potty-training stage. In the matter of elimination, he can rebel by retaining or delaying. He may also comply or he may be frustrated if he is unable. He realizes that this is his, not his mother's, and she can't forcibly take it away from him. She can only coax, plead, and threaten. His waste products are of his own making and thus receive tremendous value in the young child's mind. His way of handling mother at this stage is called the *passive-mastery* stage. He now has the upper hand. If mother's demands are too early, too strict, or too forceful, the child soon learns mastery over her by anal retention, or nongiving.

He could easily grow up to be stingy and stubborn in later life, unable to give of himself, his time, or his money. He can stir up strife in such a way that he will not be recognized as the instigator. Thus, his hostility is gratified when he becomes a passive observer of the problems he creates for other people.

We have all known or read about people who were stingy or hoarded money or other commodities. One such person is told about in the following story.

A woman known as "Madam" left a fortune in her mansion. The house, situated about two miles from the University of Virginia campus, was demolished in Charlottesville some time ago. The wrecking crews were startled to see wads of greenbacks pop out of the mortar and brick rubble. At least thirty persons reportedly discovered hundreds of dollars each and a sixteen-year-old girl found $8,000 in a rusty metal box that had been buried four feet in the ground.

Money, in denominations as big as $1,000 bills, was also found in glass jars buried in the yard, while some was molded into the plaster walls of the one-time three-story red brick house that had twenty-three bedrooms. All the bills, musty with age, were found meticulously and tightly wrapped with rubber bands.

This woman illustrates the anal retentive person. Such a person has difficulty in giving up anything.

Aggressive Behavior

From the passive-mastery stage, a baby may move to a more *aggressive-hostile-mastery* stage. Expulsion of body wastes seems to be emotionally equal to the flow of filthy words.

The desires of a baby to soil himself, his clothing, and his bedding is one way of showing his hostility. Adults who have had problems in this early stage of life are usually very hostile people.

Many people are obsessed with dirty words, dirty jokes, and obscene stories. You will notice that the words they use and the words they often paint on walls generally refer to waste products from the human body. These people are manipulative, opinionated, and argumentative. They are virtually bristling with aggressive hostility. Any kindness they show may be a reaction against their hostility; but this kindness is superficial. Eventually their hostility manifests itself to those closely associated with them. They play a double role in life. In order to be accepted, they put up the facade of a nice person, particularly to strangers.

One day an acquaintance of mine from a local university phoned for an appointment. I thought, "What could he possibly need me for?" He had always been one of the kindest and politest men I have ever known. He opened the car door for the ladies. His manners were marvelous. He abhorred violence, his language was pure, he was self-sacrificing. You could meet him early in the morning, late at night, or after a busy, disappointing, and frustrating day and he was always controlled and just the same — polite, kind, well-mannered. He seemed to take the troubles of life with such poise and grace. So his call for an appointment really had me puzzled.

For the appointment, he and his wife came together. They told me they were getting a divorce. "Why?" I asked. She said that her husband was impossible to live with. "In church or outside of the home he is gracious and loving but as soon as he walks in the door at home he is hostile and argumentative. Every discussion turns into a matching of the wits. It seems that we never argue to settle anything but I get the feeling that he simply wants to wear me down and win every point. If we ever do resolve a problem, he finds something new to master me with."

I began seeing the husband twice a week in depth therapy. His sweet exterior suddenly began to crack. He fumed and swore in the sessions. He was going to hire an attorney and really get even with a business colleague. He wanted to make him suffer. Then his anger was turned toward me. He began to hate me. He argued with me about the techniques I used with him in therapy. He wanted to fight about every little issue. I simply let him steam on, sometimes hardly saying three words in a forty-five-minute period.

Slowly his need to control every situation or person began to give way, and a weak, picked-on little boy began to appear. I found out that his brother was bigger than he was and had been a bully. His brother had had more privileges, more girl friends during adolescence, and more business success in those earlier years. As he dealt with these various feelings, he began to calm down and to be himself. He was no longer placid and became better able to assert himself. He began to express the true qualities of a husband. He no longer took out on his wife the unresolved frustrations that belonged to his relationship with his brother.

People like this may be highly regarded in the local church because of their seeming godliness, while at the same time they can be negative and rejecting of their wife and family or any friends that get too close. In a theological argument, they can never be wrong.

No amount of argument can convince them that they are wrong. They are not defending the Scriptures as life values, but using them to prove their mastery in a given situation. In their zeal for truth, we sense they have no genuine interest either in people or in the truth. Instead, their zeal is to protect their self or ego.

The "Show-off" Stage

Following this stage of aggressive behavior development, the young child enters the age of *exhibitionism*. This is the age of demonstration.

He has tremendous curiosity about bodies and sex. He delights in running around the house without clothes, much to the distress of his mother. His interest in sex is very intense. He experiences pleasure in playing with himself. In his fantasy, he has secret desires of having the parent of the opposite sex all to himself. The song "I Want a Girl Just Like the Girl That Married Dear Old Dad" displays this feeling. Young boys often say they are going to marry their mommy when they grow up. This is the child's first awareness of the other sex. These desires combined with sexual curiosity about the body of the parent of the opposite sex can cause extreme anxiety for the child. A young boy may resolve these feelings by transferring his interest from mother to daddy. He will start identifying more and more with daddy's interest in sports, work, or hobbies. In this way he is resolving his feelings of anxiety because he knows that he can't compete with daddy for mother's affections on a mature level. Subconsciously he is saying, "Since I can't beat daddy and since he could destroy me because he is bigger than I, I will become like him." Through this healthy identification, the boy child begins to become mentally as well as physically a member of the male sex.

Inability to grow beyond a desire for his mother and to identify with the father figure is one of the causes of homosexuality. The child slows down in his emotional sexual development. He is anxious and tense, frightened and suspicious.

However, if he passes through this stage successfully, he has opened the gateway to reality. He is no longer preoccupied with his own body and its needs. His sexual curiosity gives way to the latency period where all sexuality is repressed. Other interests take the place of an interest in sex, such as nature studies, hobbies, baseball, etc. Then at puberty, when bodily changes take place, sexuality is reawakened and becomes a part of the person's physical drives. Passing through the gateway to reality means that the youngster discovers other people. Puberty begins the age of social development. Not only does the boy discover girls, but he is oversensitive in desiring to conform to his peer group.

Relating to Others

The final step in maturity is epitomized by one word: *sharing*, which is the genital stage. This state brings to completion the early Oedipal stage where there was selfishness, competition, and immaturity. Instead of being self-centered, the young man is object-centered.

He has equal regard for himself and his needs and for the needs and feelings of others. He is just as concerned with the happiness, health, and sensitivities of the loved object as he is with himself.

Fixations or regressions to former stages of development instill in the person the traits that correspond to that earlier period in the child's development. For instance, the character-structure of Scrooge in Charles Dickens' *Christmas Carol* exemplifies the mastery level of life. Scrooge is stingy, self-centered, and hostile. Psychologists, through counseling, seek to remove the fears and blocks that arrested such a person on this level of development and help him move up the ladder toward unselfishness and sharing. How this process of counseling aids a person is discussed in Part 3. When a person is able to cope with the world in reality, rather than projecting his problems onto people and reacting toward them in his present life as he did toward his frustrating parents, he has come a long way toward maturity.

We might illustrate this by the story of a man who had an unresolved mother attachment. One of the most common frustrations in marital battles is the constant arguing over little things that are seen by both parties to be very important. Behind the little things is a background that husbands and wives do not understand. Consider the marriage of Bill and Susan.

> After an initial interview, it appeared that Susan was fairly well emotionally adjusted but Bill had a real hang-up that he couldn't understand. As therapy progessed, he began to talk more and more about his mother — how he loved her and how she did everything for him. His bed was made for him and his every wish or desire was met. He told me she was even jealous when he fell in love with Susan. He was her boy whom she had brought into the world.
>
> When he got married, he was unconsciously looking for an extension of his mother in his wife. Susan wanted a husband who was strong — a person she could lean on and look up to. Instead of meeting his every whim, she made demands of him. He had never learned to share but didn't realize it. In his therapy, many and varied dreams about his mother were analyzed, including the deep attachments and infantile feelings he had for her. As he saw these, he was slowly able to develop more

independence and reliance on his own talents and abilities. He learned to share with Susan and the problem was resolved.

The pattern is usually the same. Mother always did everything for her son and made no demands upon him. When he marries, he unconsciously wants these same qualities in his wife. If, however, after marriage, his wife makes demands of him, he might react with hostility. He may decide that his wife is a demanding shrew and that he should divorce her. The real problem is not that he does not have a happy, well-adjusted wife, but that she is not meeting his mother need. He does not recognize this mother-dependence in himself. All he knows is that these demands make him anxious, because they call on him to act like a man. If he could face this problem realistically, he would realize that he has an unconscious desire to remain a little, irresponsible boy, taken care of by his mother.

Sometimes a therapist must be careful not to give a person too much insight into his current problem until he is strong enough to accept the challenge to go on with emotional maturity. This is true because a person must be ready to cope with the problem; too much knowledge about himself may lead to hopelessness and a deeper emotional regression.

If a person is able and willing to gain insight into his problem, he can work through these blocks, grow up emotionally, develop a mature sense of his own masculinity, and assume his position as father in the home. This is what we mean by reality. When he discovers his problem, sees his wife as she really is, and responds toward her accordingly, he relinquishes the projections toward her that characterized the relationship toward his mother. He discovers suddenly that not all women are like his mother and that each individual needs to be understood and accepted as he or she really is.

It should be quite clear by now that the ego grows only by its contacts with people and reality. The deeper the introversion and the earlier the fixation, the weaker the ego. Introversion means that the person withdraws within himself. This is in direct proportion to how the individual sees external reality. The less he comprehends reality, the more he withdraws. And the deeper the introversion, the more psychologically sick is the person. A good strong ego grows as it experiences satisfying, emotionally involved relationships with other people. If the child is fixated at the stage where he wants his mother to himself and feels guilty and fearful in his attitude toward his father, he may grow up to be not only an overly anxious and tense adult, but also one who is not able to resolve his sexual hang-ups.

He may feel that anything that is pleasurable is wrong. If he asserts himself aggressively, he will feel as though he should be punished. Enjoying too much pleasure in any relationship carries with it a sense of guilt. He could become a masochist, that is, a person who hates himself. He judges himself and his actions too harshly. He may even subconsciously set himself up for failure, as this is a form of punishment. He unconsciously needs his troubles, and would be lost without them. This attitude will infuse his whole adult life. In his asceticism, he misses the true pleasures and enjoyments of life because of the guilt he feels he must assume. A similar development takes place in the girl child who loves her father and identifies with her mother.

The ego can be compared with the corn plant. If the latter is sheltered from the pressures of life — the wind, the rain, and the sun — it will shrivel and become brittle, and it will not produce any ears of corn. In the same way, our ego needs people, problems, and perplexities to attain a sense of accomplishment. We need to use our ego to develop our talents to help others and to branch out and try new avenues of expression. These experiences produce emotional maturity and give the individual a meaning and purpose for living.

5

How We Develop Values

While We Grow Emotionally, We Continue
to Learn New Ideas and Concepts

A BABY IS born into the world without any knowledge of right or wrong, truth or falsehood. He cannot discern a good person from a bad person. He is like a blank piece of paper until experiences begin to make impressions on him. He usually finds out the hard way that a stove is hot and medicine is bitter, or that Mary is kind but Joe is mean.

Eventually, these concepts of pleasure and pain, good and bad, become clarified. If the child matures properly, he will profit from his past experiences. The fact is, all of us should be continually learning new concepts, ideas, or values from reality experiences. It is through these life experiences that a person learns to know God. A four-year-old can stump experts with his questions about life, yet at eighty-five most of the mysteries of life are still unsolved. Maturity may not answer all questions, but it will strengthen one's faith in the abundant goodness of God.

In this chapter, we will explain how a person finds his own value system in life, so that he can deal effectively with reality. Actually, there is little about our personality that is original. Our thoughts, words, actions, and values are all various combinations of acquired learning. We obey others or we observe and imitate them in their ability to cope with reality. As we incorporate these observations or instructions, they become our value system and help to shape our own unique personality.

Our First Teachers

Since a baby has no sense of values, he soon starts learning his parents' values. The parents teach him their own value system both by their actions and their words. They communicate very early to the small child the regulations of the household. For example, the child learns not to drink pop in the living room, not to call people bad names, not to fight, what time to go to bed, etc. As he grows, he learns that he is expected to clean up his own messes, go to school five days a week, eat everything on his plate, say "please" and "thank you." He learns manners and morals as well as acceptable behavior patterns from his parents and siblings.

If the family is a Christian family, special emphasis may be placed on church attendance, daily prayer, and Bible study. The parents and the church may spend a great deal of time teaching him about the love of Christ. He may be taught that it is wrong to smoke, steal, lie, or drink alcoholic beverages. He is taught to honor his parents. If the parents are consistent, the child will better understand what their values are and will be more ready to accept them.

After the child learns his parents' standards and values, he begins to imitate them. For example, when he is about to touch a pretty vase, he may tell himself not to, instead of waiting for mother to say, "No, no." At this age children love to imitate their parents. Small girls play "dress up" in mother's clothes and small boys pack tool kits around or drive little play cars in imitation of daddy.

Children have a tremendous capacity for imitation. They can mimic manners, words, and actions quite easily. An older brother learns to control his little brother by acting like his parents and using the language they use for discipline. This imitation becomes an identification with the parent because either the child fears or is seeking love and approval. In other words, the child who is fearful of father's discipline will more readily identify with him because he knows he can't win, so the idea is "If you can't lick them, join them." By his identifying with daddy's rules, the relationship between father and son is strengthened. On the other hand, the identification may be made out of love. The child wants to please the parents because he loves them. This is demonstrated by the words of Jesus: "If you love me, you will do what I command" (John 14:15).

"Not-Quite" Stage

As the young child grows and begins to experience his own identity, he starts to examine what he has learned. He may begin to question his parents or try to discover their reasons for making certain rules. Parents of Christian young people are fearful of this "rebellion," but it is a perfectly natural stage in the child's development. Adolescence is called the "not-quite" stage, because the child is not really a child anymore, but he is not an adult, either. There is a need for the youngster to rebel, for he is learning independence and is striving to become an individual, not just be a carbon copy of his parents.

A number of years ago when my children were small, I decided to put together from a kit a forty-six-foot-long patio covering on the back of our house. I could have done it much faster by myself, but we decided to make it a family project to give us a chance to do something together.

After we started, one of the boys began following the second step of the directions before the first part was completed. I explained to him he would end up having to do it over again. He got angry and told me he knew what he was doing and that he didn't need any help from me.

This typically shows how a child tries to assert his independence.

Also at this stage of life, the youngster's peer group is very important to him. He wants to be accepted by his friends as well as by his parents, and where there are different values there are bound to be conflicts. The youngster is thinking through the parental value system and comparing it to the value system of his peer group or to the value system of the group's parents. He listens to what other parents say to their children when he is in another home. He likes the way his parents handle one thing, but he prefers the actions of the other parents in another situation. His need to be accepted is so great that if his parents' standards are too divergent from those of his peer group, he is in a dilemma. He must decide whether to follow his parents' standards or forsake them in order to be accepted by his own group. In short, he must accept or reject certain values that he has learned. If the parents' standards seem right to him, he will align himself with these and find a group in society that more adequately fits his needs.

For instance, if his crowd is too "worldly" in talk and action, he may forsake that group and join a church group whose values more closely resemble those of his parents. At this point, he has come full circle. His parents' standards are now his own standards. This value system is now his very own, for he has tested and approved it as a way of life for him. On the other hand, he may brand his parents' values as too narrow, and reject their standards. Then he has to incorporate standards and values from other experiences. Either way, the young adult develops his own value system.

Some Things May Need Change

Throughout a person's lifetime, his value system is subject to change. At forty a parent may realize he was too strict with the oldest child and become more lenient with the younger children. Another parent may have decided that all movies are bad and that his children will not be allowed to attend them, only to be confronted with the issue of movies on television. At this point he might become more flexible in his position, either because of exposure or because of social pressure. A healthy sense of personal identity makes a person flexible enough to accept changes in an ever-changing life situation.

This flexibility prevents a person from becoming so rigid in his views that he becomes unrealistic in his relationship to the modern world. Religious people often severely criticize psychologists on the grounds that they do not condemn wrong conduct when it is divulged in the therapeutic situation. They feel that silence on the part of the analyst condones wrong actions.

When I was training to become a psychologist, we often watched the training psychologist work with a patient, observing the procedure through a one-way window that appeared to be a mirror in the other room. The room was wired for sound, so we could also hear what was said. One day a group of ministers was present to watch a session from the viewing room. Coincidentally, on that particular day the patient was a girl nineteen years of age whose father was a minister.

She began venting her hatred for the church and told how much she hated her parents for cramming all their ideas down her throat. She went on and on, even to a point of profanity. She said they never allowed her to give her views on anything. She didn't even feel ilke a person. She wondered how she could ever know what she believed herself if she couldn't talk about it freely to anyone. During the hour, about all the psychologist said was, "Um, uh, ha." At the end of the hour, all he said was, "How do you feel now?" After the girl left, the psychologist came into the room, and the hour was discussed. One minister severely criticized the psychologist, saying, "Boy, if I'd been in there, I would have really set that girl straight." To this the psychologist replied, "She had that all her life. Apparently, it didn't work. Maybe this time she needs somebody who will just listen."

Most psychologists concede that it is impossible to keep from influencing a person's value system. Even in being silent or at times pointing out a resistant area of life, the psychologist is changing that person's value system, hence his life pattern. The psychologist is trained not to condemn so that the patient will feel accepted and be able to relate with the therapist. Through this identification, the patient will better understand why he feels guilty, hostile, or depressed, and will be better able to resolve these feelings. It is this identification that encourages the patient to develop a healthy pattern of growth toward maturity.

"Stop-and-Go" Lights

These psychological principles need to be applied within the realm of Christianity, especially as they relate to the value structure and performance of the church. Since life begins with God, it seems logical that He knows best what are our needs, our limitations, our weaknesses, our temptations, our talents, and our strengths. Certainly, He knows the things that will bring us enduring happiness on earth and eternal happiness in heaven.

To illustrate, it is reasonable to assume that if a man owns a new Ford automobile, he should comply with the rules of maintenance that have been published in the Ford owner's manual by the Ford Motor Company. Now the man may choose to disregard these rules and decide that the car will work fine without those recommended services. Performance problems may not show up for many thousands of miles, but sooner or later the owner of the car will discover that the manufacturer knew what he was talking about. Engines often wear out long before they should because they are not cared for properly.

God also has laid down certain moral laws for men to live by and these laws may seem overwhelming and unnecessary. But He gives us these laws for our own good. "His commands are not burdensome" (1 John 5:3). God is not trying to dampen our pleasure, but He is concerned about our genuine happiness. Man needs to know and understand these laws written in the Bible, so that he can build a value system that will reconcile him to his Creator. There is no fulfilled life — no life worth living — apart from God.

God brings to us great principles that are meant for our happiness. "He who commits adultery has no sense; he who does it destroys himself" (Proverbs 6:32). The modern "free love" philosophy that states that "any act is all right as long as it doesn't hurt anyone else" is false. Immoral acts always hurt someone else besides hurting the person who commits them, although he might not recognize it at the time. A perfect example is that of Sally and Mike.

"We love each other; we want to express that love sexually; nobody else is being hurt, so why shouldn't we go ahead?" said a young man of nineteen to his girl friend. A few months later Sally came to my office broken and confused. She said that Mike and she had engaged in sex relations and at the time she could not see how anybody could be hurt. She had thought that that idea had just been a carry-over from her Puritan past. "Now," she said, "I am beginning to see it differently. As soon as Mike got what he wanted, he no longer seemed to be interested in marrying me. I also began to become confused as to my feeling about him. Did I really love him for himself or were we just using each other? Another thing that bothers me now is whether I could trust Mike to be faithful to me after we were married. I never thought I would be guilty about this but now that I have done it I can see I really am. I'm terribly upset."

The effect of these acts may not show up immediately, but the disintegration of the person's self-image and character occur eventually.

Fortunately, God realizes our weaknesses. We may get ourselves into the worst of situations, but isn't the forgiveness of Christ wonderful? He tells us in His Word: "My grace is sufficient for you" (2 Corinthians 12:9).

One of the complaints about the Christian value system is that it is so narrow that it does not allow a person to function as a normal, thinking human being. Critics complain that if a person follows this value system to the letter, he will be stunted in his emotional growth. Jesus warned against such false teachers who in their own way may be well-meaning: "'They worship me in vain; their teachings are but rules made by men. You have let go of the commands of God and are holding on to the traditions of men.' And he said to them: 'You have a fine way of setting aside the commands of God in order to observe your own traditions! . . . Thus you nullify the word of God by your tradition that you have handed down. And you do many things like that'" (Mark 7:7-9, 13).

We can say that obeying the true laws of God taught in the Bible will not make a person emotionally ill but will produce a reliable standard on which people can depend as a guideline for their own best interests. Thus, any Victorian standard that is a tradition of one particular group from its inception and not found in the Bible must be taken for tradition and not taught as gospel truth.

Take Only What Applies to You

Another aspect of the Christian dilemma lies in interpreting the minister's words. He preaches the truth as he sees it to different people with different needs. The Word of God contains many messages for different people. Some members of the congregation need comfort, others need doctrine, while others need to be convicted of their sins. Every time the pastor speaks, he has before him all of these different people with their individual needs and problems. Obviously, the pastor cannot meet all these needs in any one sermon, so it becomes the responsibility of the individual to decide how much the message applies to him.

Many a pastor has presented a message on "giving," only to be criticized by the best tither in the church. In a spirit of hostility this man resents the implication that he is not giving enough. He feels he can't give more and shouldn't be expected to. Obviously, in this case the sermon was not meant for this particular man. When the pastor invites the wayward to come to Christ, he is speaking to those in the congregation who are not Christians.

Applying the psychological principles cited, we would conclude that the Christian with a healthy value system would discern whether the message applies to him or not. This means that a Christian must develop his own value system and reject what doesn't pertain to him. In addition, he has a right to expect accurate Bible interpretation from the pulpit. If the pastor says, "You are not a good Christian unless you pass out tracts," he is in error, for not all Christians have the courage or the ability to pass out tracts.

If a man has a weak, sensitive ego and is plagued by guilt, then a church that overstresses sin and guilt instead of joy and happiness will produce more of a sense of guilt in the parishioner, often with devastating results. There are times when the congregation, individually or as a body, should speak to the "fire-and-brimstone" type of preacher who is always harping on the subject. Certainly God never intended Christians to become guilt-laden and emotionally ill by attending church. Even if the Christian is being convicted of some sin in his life, the sermon should not drive him from God, but should enlighten him, so he can understand his problem and better relate to the Lord and others.

A woman once came to me complaining that she got a headache every Sunday morning. She said, "I sincerely love the Lord, but I can't go to church. I feel guilty about it and wonder if I'm committing the unpardonable sin." After telling me her story, she felt so relieved that she decided to try church again the following Sunday. Part way through the message she couldn't take it, left the sanctuary, and sat crying on the steps to the balcony. One of the Christian workers in the church came to ask what was wrong. She said, "I just can't take the pastor's sermons. They are always warning us about sin, making us feel as though we are never yielded. Frankly, I get so depressed." The Christian worker said that he felt it should be brought to the attention of the pastor. This he did. The pastor replied, "It is nothing more than the conviction of sin and she is fighting the surrender of her life to the Lord." Nearer to the truth was the fact that the minister had his own problem. He was always negative and hostile. This woman brought me the bulletin from her church the following week. I noted that the title of the morning sermon was "The Judgments of God," the evening message was "Sodom and Gomorrah," and Wednesday night's topic was "Demon Possession." Here was a woman who needed to be built up in the faith and brought to a rational, reasonable approach to the realm of spiritual responsibility.

We should realize that the pastor also can have his emotional hang-ups. For instance, he may overemphasize morals and constantly harass everyone to "get right" with God, when in reality he may only be projecting his guilt complex on the congregation.

"What you are to be you are now becoming," said a famous British Christian. This is true of all maturing Christians. An emotionally healthy person is able to broaden, deepen, and refine his own value system by applying, deleting, or including new data into an organized, well-integrated value structure that assists him in adequately relating to circumstances, persons, and God.

6

People With a Weak Identity

How People With Low Self-Esteem React

WE HAVE BEEN discussing the need for a strong self-concept in order to meet the demands of life. Let us now examine the signs in people who have a weak self-concept. The characteristic may take several forms: psychotic, neurotic, and regressive behavior.

Since the ego must deal with reality, we can state that all forms of psychosis demonstrate the most severe ego loss and disturbance. There are numerous examples of people who go berserk with no apparent control over their behavior. Some are not even aware of their actions. We think of the man who killed eight Chicago nurses and of the man who climbed the tower on the University of Texas campus and shot seventeen people with a rifle.

The weak ego of both of these men caused them to act out internal conflicts on a grand scale. They probably did not know their victims, nor did they have any personal grudges against them. Usually victims of such violence are complete strangers to the murderers. The man who killed the nurses had a fantasy of hate toward his own mother, so he "destroyed" her eight times by killing the women. He had lost contact with reality and this caused him to act out his hostility against society in such a bizarre way. A person who acts out his hostility in such a manner is suffering from intense ego disintegration.

If You Hear Voices

Another psychotic manifestation of ego disintegration is hallucination. The person who suffers from hallucination may hear voices talking to him. To him these voices are real. They may indicate love or hate toward him. He invents his own reality through voices and cannot be convinced that they do not exist. A person can also experience visual hallucinations in which he sees people or things. In either case, the hallucinations seem very real, although there is no appropriate external stimulus.

46

Actually, the person has lost contact with reality and the hallucination is his attempt to regain real objects by creating them in fantasy. He talks to them and they talk to him. Whether they are kind or severe depends upon his own superego, which he has projected to the external world. His conscience becomes a person *outside* himself in fantasy and this person punishes him or loves him for his behavior. "I hate him" becomes "He hates me." The person with this malady has lost his own sense of identity and simply projects his feelings onto the object of his hallucination. This, of course, relieves him of responsibility for his behavior or his impulses: "I am innocent; he is bad."

What Is a Neurosis?

In a neurosis, the ego has not lost contact with reality but is suffering from a "free-floating" anxiety in which the true self is threatened. When this anxiety becomes too great, the person may fear insanity. Many symptoms may be evident. Extreme crying or laughing without apparent cause may be signs of ego weakness and are methods of releasing anxiety. The following story is an illustration of free-floating anxiety.

> A young woman sat in my office and described her anxiety like this: "It's like something terrible is about to happen and I don't know what it is. I'm frightened, but I don't know why. At times I just start crying and I don't feel sad about anything particularly. Then suddenly I may start laughing and not be able to stop. It is like you are floating out there loose in thin air. At times I feel as though I am going to burst, fly apart, or go to pieces. I even break out into a cold sweat and hot and cold flashes." Even as she talked I could see her body get rigid and her tears mix with occasional laughter. She shifted back and forth in her seat and jumped every time there was a noise outside. As she talked faster and faster, I could see that her words were nothing but a frantic attempt to get help. She seemed afraid to come to the appointment and equally afraid to leave. She said that she wanted to call me between visits to get reassurance that I was there. "I just need to hang onto someone all the time," she said.

Another sign of a weak ego is excessive daydreaming. The daydreamer is always building castles in the air and imagining that he is in a glorious position of power or potency. He may dream that he is a president, a movie star, a sports hero, or a sought-after Adonis. Since his ego is not strong enough to deal with reality, he compensates for his inferiority in work or in love by creating his own world where he is always winning, wanted, and wonderful.

Unfortunately, some people mistakenly use the spiritual dimension in this way. By contemplation about God under the guise of walking with God, they build a world in which they are sheltered from all storms of life. Some of these people even enter monastic life with the apparent motive of spiritual devotion, whereas in reality they are seeking someone to take care of them, to make all their decisions, to shelter them from a cruel, competitive world, to pay their bills, to feed them, and to guarantee them lifetime care. This is a misuse of faith. Jesus prayed that His disciples should not be taken out of the world but be kept from evil while they are in the world (John 17:15).

Another sign of a weak self-concept is seen in the impulsive neurotic who acts on an impulse before he thinks. This person acts and reacts too quickly. He cannot contain his feeling until he has thought it through. This may be true of his temper, his eating, or his buying. He can see only the present moment and his immediate need and cannot withhold the desire for instant satisfaction. He cannot wait for a more practical solution in the future.

What Is a Regression?

Another sign of a weak self-concept is the evidence of regression. At the slightest pressure of everyday circumstances, the regressive person tends to withdraw into a shell or exhibits childlike demands or behavior. Every normal person tends to regress under severe pressure, such as the death of a loved one, but he bounces back and adjusts to reality with full use of his talents and faculties. The person with a weak ego may also bounce back, but it is a much slower process. He may even stay at a fixed point, psychologically, back in childhood where life was safer. He may resent anyone who tries to move him beyond that point.

You've Heard of "Defense Mechanisms"?

A person who has a weak ego must find some way to defend himself against anxiety. Defenses are a good thing. We all need them in order to cope with the pressures of the outside world. However, they may be used in a wrong way. For instance, a young child lies because he can't stand the pressure of facing the truth.

Someone once gave a good definition of a defense: "It is the ability to handle and organize frustrations so I can cope with the problems of my life." Defenses can fulfill a vital purpose because they help the ego to deal more effectively with reality.

When a person has a weak ego he may rely upon what the psychologist calls "neurotic defenses." These defenses are the abuse or the failure of a normal defense.

A good illustration of a defense of a neurotic sort may be that of a certain auto mechanic as he repairs cars at a dealership which pays mechanics by commission. The mechanic thinks to himself, "Wow, I have to pay out forty-two dollars next week for that TV repair job! The guy said seven parts had gone bad — the gyp artist! Well, I'll think up some extra repairs on some cars today to make up my loss because of the TV. The customers can afford it, anyway. Man, I wish I had this dealership. I'd get me that big sailboat I saw. Oh well, I'm doing okay. I wouldn't want to stay around and work so many late hours like the boss does."

Let's analyze this man's thought, noting the defenses. There was first, *projection* — that is, he called the TV repairman a crook when he is one himself. He *compensated* for his probable loss by planning to get extra money on needless parts and repairs. He *rationalized* his behavior by assuming that the car owners could afford the cost. He fantasized by *daydreaming* about owning the business. Then he used the defense of *isolation*, or the "sour grapes" technique of telling himself that he really didn't want the business, which he couldn't have anyhow. (The "sour grapes" phrase comes from the old story about the fox who tried several times to jump up to grab some grapes, which were too high. So, the fox left, telling himself that he wouldn't want them anyhow, because they were probably sour.)

Do these defenses sound rather familiar to you? They ought to, because we all use them in various ways from time to time.

Perhaps you may be saying at this point, "What kind of defense is sinful and when is it neurotic?" For instance, let us take the above-mentioned defense of *isolation*. A person may isolate himself from a problem that may be too great for him at a given moment. For example, a salesman after a hard day's work may isolate the problem he is having with a neighbor because the day's work is all he can take. Here the defense worked in his favor and served a good purpose. But other people may isolate themselves from worship in God's house because they don't want to face something that is wrong in their lives.

So a defense is right or wrong, depending on how it is used.

In the Bible we find many examples of people whose strong egos were weakened, and they reacted abnormally. When Adam and Eve fell into sin, their relationship with God was broken. They first had lost their divine object. "The man and his wife hid themselves from the presence of the Lord God among the trees of the garden" (Genesis 3:8). This is the first implication of guilt in human existence. "I heard the sound of thee in the garden, and I was afraid" (Genesis 3:10). Here we have the first record of fear in human beings.

We also find the illustration of the use of an ego defense. "The woman whom thou gavest to be with me, she gave me fruit of the tree, and I ate" (Genesis 3:12). Here again we have a graphic illustration of the *projection* defense. Feeling anxious about his own guilt, Adam defended himself against it by projecting his guilt upon the wife God gave him. Actually, he blamed God for giving him a bad wife and the bad wife for tempting him. Being defensive, he was not willing to accept any responsibility for his wrongful behavior.

Cain used the defense mechanisms of *rationalization* and *denial* when he could not stand his own jealousy because God accepted Abel's offering and rejected his. He acted out impulsively and murdered his brother. When he was asked, "Where is Abel thy brother?" he rationalized his action by saying, "Am I my brother's keeper?" (Genesis 4:9). Instead of accepting responsibility for what he had done, he shifted the responsibility by rationalizing, "I am not responsible for what happens to him."

When Abraham was in Egypt with his wife Sarah, fearing that the Egyptians would kill him to abduct his wife, he used the defense mechanism of *denial*. He advised her to deny her true relationship to him. "Say you are my sister, that it may go well with me because of you, and that my life may be spared on your account" (Genesis 12:13). Isaac, Abraham's son, in identifying with his father, repeated the same response by saying his beautiful wife was his sister when he was confronted by Abimelech. "So Abimelech called Isaac, and said, 'Behold, she is your wife; how then could you say, "She is my sister"?' Isaac said to him, 'Because I said, "Lest I die because of her"'" (Genesis 26:9).

All defense mechanisms devised by the ego are used to prevent the person from feeling too much anxiety and guilt. There are many more than those illustrated here. Our purpose in this chapter is only to demonstrate several and to show how the ego uses them.

When Are Defenses Normal?

You may feel at this point that defense mechanisms are bad or sinful. As pointed out, this is not necessarily true. The defenses mentioned are normal in childhood development. Without good defenses and the ability to use them, the ego is in danger. Every person needs to strengthen his defenses in order to cope with anxiety. The defense structure is sick only when a defense is abused or the defenses used are too immature. For instance, if a person *projects* all his problems onto another person, he will never mature because he takes no responsibility for his own actions. Therefore, he cannot resolve his behavior problems if he does not accept them as being his own. How a person may project onto another is seen by the following typical story.

7

When We Face Anxiety

The More Severe Disorders That Threaten Self

EARLIER WE DISCLOSED that in most cases mental disorders were nothing but exaggerated defensive maneuvers conceived by the ego to deal with excessive amounts of anxiety. The mechanisms of defense that we dealt with in the preceding chapter play an important role in the abnormal condition manifested in a person who is suffering from a specific mental disorder. Why one person unconsciously chooses one form of defense and another person a different defense is not fully understood today.

All we can say is that no two people are exactly alike genetically nor do they have exactly the same environment or background. Parents are perplexed when they see two of their children develop such different character traits. They can't understand how two youngsters with the same background can behave so differently. But no two people have the same background even though they share the identical parents, home, and schools.

All Different

To illustrate, let us imagine a home with three children — two boys and a girl. Joe, the oldest, is twelve; Jerry, the middle boy, is ten; and Jill, the girl, is seven. Jerry has to compete with a big brother who is stronger, is given more privileges, and earns more money. Jerry probably has to wear the clothes that his big brother has outgrown. His sense of hate and rivalry show up in his competitive behavior. He is always trying to keep up, to prove himself. He may be loud and boisterous or very aggressive. He notices that this type of behavior gets attention from his parents, even if the attention is in the form of punishment. Maybe when Jill was born, all the love and attention that Jerry once enjoyed passed on to her. He feels cheated and hostile. In addition, his daddy had always wanted a daughter and unconsciously rejected the boys because they were not girls. Both Joe and Jerry could grow up feeling rejected by their father, while Jill feels especially close to him.

There may be more complications. Mother may clash with Joe, the oldest boy, because he acts like his father, for whom she feels hostility because he is too passive and leaves her with too much of the responsibility of running a home and rearing a family. So she pays more attention to Jerry, and if Joe senses her favoritism, he will resent it. The situation is not the same at school, either. Joe's I.Q. is below normal, so he can't compete academically. His teacher favors bright students; so he feels left out and rejected by her. Jerry, however, is a gifted child; so he competes with his older brother and attempts to beat him by excelling in school.

Then there is Jill. She resents being treated like the baby of the family. She also has a problem relating to other children outside the home. She is pampered and protected in the home, but she is just another child to her peer group. She has a problem adjusting to reality outside of her home environment.

At this point it should be apparent that even children in the same family don't have the same background or constitutional framework. Physical ability, mental ability, placement in the family, sex, and sibling rivalry all contribute to personality development and consequent behavior. Because their experiences have not been the same, the children mentioned may develop different ways of defending themselves against their anxieties and adjustment problems.

Jill may become a mother's girl and withdraw from other relationships by detaching herself from people. If she shuts people off from herself emotionally, then they can't hurt her. She may become an avid animal-lover, since she knows that animals don't talk back and can't hurt her feelings. Jerry may become very aggressive by telling people off, by getting into fights, or even by breaking the law. He may mask his deep inferiority and his threatened sense of manhood by compensation. He will try to prove himself a man and feed his ego by being tough. However, little ego strength is developed, since he never deals directly with his sense of inferiority because he never faces it.

Because of his intellectually unproductive life, Joe may feel inferior in the home, and may desperately attempt to find approval outside the home. But since everybody else has different tastes and attitudes, he cannot meet all these conflicting demands to get approval. He may decide, therefore, that he is a bad guy, turn his hostility inward, decide that nobody likes him, and become a depressive. Now all of us can see some of these tendencies within ourselves because we move through these different phases in childhood development. Only the severity of the symptoms indicate an abnormal adjustment to life.

Types of Anxiety

This story shows how different children are treated in a given home. Anxiety states, hostility, etc., may be developed early in life and these can bring on deep and serious psychological disorders later in life. It is important for us to examine these specific mental diseases, noting their special implications for the Christian.

Anxiety is a signal to the ego that something from the unconscious that is painful to the ego is about to come into consciousness. It is felt that some unknown evil, danger, or threat is about to occur. It may be expressed by an individual in these words, "I feel like I'm coming unglued. I'm scared and don't know why."

It is the excess amount of anxiety that makes it abnormal. Without the proper amount of anxiety there would not be motivation to work, to avoid danger, to finish school, or to compete. Proper anxiety makes us aware of really dangerous situations, and enables us to protect ourselves. For example, a man would not jump away from a car approaching him if he weren't anxious for his life. However, if a person feels anxious, thinking that he is about to be destroyed or hurt when there is no reason in reality for this feeling, then he is suffering from abnormal anxiety.

Abnormal or pathological anxiety can be divided into three different categories. First, there is the *acute anxiety state*. This condition comes on a person very suddenly, without any warning. It is very intense, and is usually short-lived. The person may be affected while walking down the street, folding letters at the office or relaxing at home. Symptoms will be the feeling of going to pieces, bursting, or flying apart, and may be accompanied by hot and cold flashes or profuse perspiration. This acute anxiety usually disappears as suddenly as it comes on. However, the affected person may develop a fear of a repeated attack.

Secondly, there is the *anxiety-tension state*. In this condition, the anxiety is comparatively high all the time. There is a constant state of uneasiness and apprehension. It usually covers a general period of time. For instance, a person who moves to a strange city away from all his relatives and friends may suffer from this chronic state. After an adjustment to the new place or a return to the original environment, the condition may disappear entirely.

Third, there is the *anxiety neurosis,* formerly referred to as anxiety hysteria. This state is rather permanent with the person most of his life and remains constant regardless of circumstances or living arrangements. The people suffering from this condition can't remember a day in their life that they didn't feel filled with tension. Some of the symptoms include irritability, rapid mood changes, depression, and problems relating to people. Their mental life may manifest poor attention span, concentration, and memory, with resulting work problems. Physically, they may be plagued with shortness of breath, heart palpitation, chest restriction, fatigue, faintness, perspiration, and facial blushing. They may develop tics or tremors and find themselves easily startled. The main defense manifested in anxiety neurosis is pure repression, which simply means keeping the thought out of consciousness. Behind each of these anxiety states is a threatened ego.

Mind Over Matter

Frequently, anxiety may help to produce physical problems in the body. When the psychoanalyst speaks of hysteria, he is usually referring to the phenomenon known as *conversion hysteria*. This "conversion" has nothing to do with spiritual conversion. It refers to the condition in which a person converts anxiety into physical symptoms. In a sense, it is as if the mind gets tired of worrying and presents the problem to the body. We see several important phenomena in this conversion reaction.

First, there is a discharge of anxiety when it is converted into a physical symptom, since this relieves some of the anxiety. Secondly, the symptom is always related to the repression. A patient's arm may develop a paralysis for which the doctor can find no organic cause. Thirdly, and closely connected with the others, is the conversion symptom that helps maintain the repression. A person with low back pains may be harboring a hidden desire to be loved and cared for. With this symptom he will receive attention from the doctor, his family, and friends. He may have unconsciously chosen this particular symptom because the back is thought of as bearing the burden of weight. So with the backache, he fosters his dependency needs and receives the sympathy from those that are close to him. Let us take the case of Lucy.

Lucy came to me one day terribly distraught because her doctor had recommended psychological help. She felt that he was wrong. She thought her problem was only physical. "It must be high blood pressure, the beginning of a tumor, or some special neurological maladjustment," she thought. After extensive X-rays and other physical tests, no physical basis for her illness could be found. I asked Lucy to simply tell me a bit about herself, and in the ensuing visits she began to verbalize her feelings freely. As she did, she noticed that her headaches were greatly relieved, but between the visits they would come often. (One of the most common maladies is the migraine headache. Probably more pills have been taken to deal with this problem than with any other physical illness.)

One day she had the feeling she was confessing something that she felt guilty about but didn't know what it was. As she talked, she remembered the time when her brother went through a phase of constant picking on her when she was in the seventh grade. He pinched her, poked fun at her, told her she was holy and that no boy would ever like her. Her mother had told her that it was a sin to ever hate anyone and she felt guilty for these bad feelings about her brother. It was just after this time that she remembered having her first headaches.

During counseling she began reliving some of her hostile feelings toward her brother. She felt relieved. But then guilt came over her, and even though her mother was now dead, it was like her voice warning her. She panicked at the thought that her mother would not love and approve of her.

Here are some of the clinical dynamics of her psychologically induced headache. Tension caused by hostility produced the headache. The headache also caused suffering. She needed the suffering as a punishment for hating her brother. She was a bad girl. We might ask why was the head chosen and not some other part of the body. The conflict and symbolism of the problem was in her mind so that part of the body suffered.

There are many forms of conversion reaction and each has a symbolical meaning. Conversion hysteria may also involve stomach disorders, intestinal trouble, and skin rashes. If the symptom gets too close to consciousness, it may manifest itself by switching to another part of the body or to another organ. This may also be illustrated by a person with an immobile arm. A paralysis for which there is no physical cause may be the distortion and displacement of one's hostile, unconscious wish to kill his father. Thus an arm receives the hostility in order to keep the person from performing the violent act. By converting the conflict into a physical symptom he distorts the undesirable hostile wish and displaces it into the body. "I am not angry; I have a physical problem."

Phobias Galore

Phobias, too, are often connected with anxiety states. There are hundreds of them. A phobia is an attempt to reduce internally generated tension by displacement, projection, and avoidance.

One common phobia is *acrophobia*, or the fear of height. This fear is perhaps expressed in the popular nursery rhyme, "Humpty Dumpty sat on the wall, Humpty Dumpty had a great fall . . ." We do not know what was in the writer's mind, but back of the ideal may have been such a fear of falling. People with this phobia stay away from mountain tops, airplanes, the tops of tall buildings, or any other high place. Any place that might cause anxiety is shunned. In the unconscious, there is a symbolic meaning connected with this fear. The real fear is falling in self-esteem, falling out of favor with parents, falling morally, or fear of self-destruction because of the impulse to fly away from troubles by jumping.

Claustrophobia is the fear of closed places. People with claustrophobia can't stand being boxed in. They are especially terrified of small places like elevators or closets. In the unconscious there is the fear of being hemmed in with no way of escape from dangerous impulses, or the fear of being left alone.

Agoraphobia is the fear of open places. Unconsciously, people with this phobia have deep dependency needs. They are afraid to go too far from home or to have too much freedom. Buildings provide a structure for protection. Without these structures, they fear they will not be able to control their impulses.

Another common phobia is *zoophobia,* or the fear of animals. Unconsciously, the fear of a sibling or a parent may be transferred to an animal. This enables the patient to love the parent and project the hostility or fear onto the animal. In this way he is able to keep the parent in a good solid relationship and project the hostility he feels toward the parent onto the animal.

We may illustrate this in another way. A man who is deeply inhibited sexually may fear animals because he cannot cope with their uninhibited sexual behavior in public places.

It is important to understand that a phobia is a phobia only when there is no reason in reality for such a feeling. A person who fears dogs because he was severely bitten in earlier life is not exhibiting a phobia but is reacting to a real experience.

"Dr. Jekyll and Mr. Hyde"

Another way the ego defends itself against excessive anxiety is by the *dissociative reaction.* In this condition, the patient attempts to escape reality by repressing entire episodes of his life from consciousness. This may take the form of the simple amnesias by which the person is unable to remember simple facts about his life, such as his name, address, or age.

Or, as in the *fugue* state, a person may take physical flight, wandering for days or even weeks, and then suddenly wake up in some strange place completely unaware of how he got there.

The most severe dissociative state is the "multiple personality." Here the person literally separates one part of his personality from the other. He becomes a "Dr. Jekyll and Mr. Hyde." One part of his personality seems to personify the id (physical drives) and the other, the superego (conscience). Since the patient cannot reconcile the two, he may develop two distinct personalities that alternate in consciousness, each taking over conscious control of the person for a different period of time. He yields to the demands of the one that is stronger at a given time, and then alternates to the other.

Charles had acquired a taste for alcohol when he was a child. His father had let him taste beer when he was only ten. He said he found that alcohol helped him forget his troubles and when he was uptight, it acted like a wonderful tranquilizer. At seventeen, he joined a very rigid, severe religious sect and felt terribly troubled about his addiction to alcohol. At times he really felt very close to God as though his thirst for alcohol was completely gone. Then suddenly his craving for it reappeared. "I want to live my religion but I can't. I use profane language and call everybody at church hypocrites. It is like I can't get myself together. I live at one extreme or the other. I can't stop living this double life. When my need for drink seems to be satisfied, I then get real religious and when I have gotten the religious satisfaction for my resolved guilt, the booze appears again."

Unable to resolve this conflict, Charles slowly developed two totally different, alternating personalities. We shall call them "Bad Charles" and "Good Charles." On the days when he was "Good Charles," he was religious, mannerly, polite, self-sacrificing, and a teetotaler. Suddenly, his whole personality would change to that of "Bad Charles." He would drink heavily, cuss and swear, deride his religion, and become sexually immoral. After a period of time he became "Good Charles" again.

In the ensuing months of therapy he was able to accept the two parts of his nature and integrate them so that he could become a whole person.

The overly suspicious person may represent another type of mental illness called paranoia. The person with a paranoid personality doesn't trust people.

One day a mother brought her twenty-two-year-old son to the office. "He desperately needs help," she exclaimed. Moments later her son, a shabbily dressed, long-haired youth sat in my office. He immediately wanted to know if the place was bugged. "What are those little buttons on the wall for? Do you have concealed microphones in here? Can anybody hear me talking in the outside office?"

The closer people try to get to this kind of person, the more suspicious he becomes. In severe states of paranoid psychosis, the patient may believe everyone is out to get him. He may believe that people hate him and are trying to destroy him. He has delusions of persecution. He handles his own tension and hostility toward people by believing they have hostility towards him, rather than he toward them. Instead of admitting that he would like to destroy other people, he imagines that they are out to destroy him, thus alleviating his own sense of guilt for his feelings.

Obsessives Think a Lot Without Feeling

The *obsessive-compulsive neurosis* is another type of defense structure against anxiety. An obsession is a thought that dominates a person's thinking. He can't get rid of it. A compulsion is a repetitious act that is consciously nonsensical even to the person performing it; for example, never stepping on a crack in the sidewalk or always putting on the left shoe first. The person always feels compelled to repeat the act. If he fails to do so, he develops anxiety. In short, the obsessive-compulsive personality attempts to avoid tension by such acts. The activity of this kind of ritualistic thinking keeps him from facing his underlying feelings. If he does excessive thinking, he will wear out his mind, just as a hard run around the block will physically tire a person. In this condition, the mental obsession becomes supreme and the person who has a more severe disorder will use this device to stay away from emotional involvement with people.

Some of the characteristics of this type of illness are excessive doubting and brooding. The person spends hours debating the pros and cons of a decision but never reaches a conclusion. He doubts that psychology can help him. He even doubts his faith and the assurance of his salvation. He also doubts his memory and is troubled by ritualistic or obsessive behavior.

He may go through elaborate details in dressing and bathing. He may be "nasty clean." The bookshelves, pictures, draperies, and tablecloths must hang evenly. If this condition becomes severe, he may not be able to control his compulsions and must, therefore, wash his hands many times a day. He may compulsively count objects such as telephone poles, cars in a parking lot, tiles in the floor, members in the church choir, or the organ pipes. He may be mortified by impulses to blaspheme God or kill his child. He experiences great guilt about his feelings and broods more and more about his spiritual life. He feels conflict between aggression and passivity, cruelty and gentleness, filthiness and cleanliness, order and disorder, masculinity and femininity, and right and wrong.

If this neurosis is not too deeply ingrained, he may be a good businessman or a scientist excelling in mathematics and technology. He is usually highly intelligent and earns a good income. He relates to people when playing a role but is terribly frustrated as a person. On the surface, he is kind and gentle, but deep down he is always threatened and hostile.

Depression That Lingers

Another familiar type of emotional disturbance is *depression*. There is such a thing as normal depression in everyone's life. The loss of a loved one because of death, desertion, or divorce is bound to be accompanied by depression. Mourning is the psychological healing process that follows the loss of a love object. Loss of power, prestige, property, money, beauty, or health may bring about depression, too. For parents to experience mild depression when the children grow up and leave home is normal. Women often experience severe depression after a hysterectomy because they fear the loss of their femininity, sexual attraction, or reproductive capacity.

Someone has described depression as the "loss syndrome." Depression becomes pathological or a mental illness when the affected person is unable to recover from the loss. In the case of the death of a loved one, if the surviving person is unable to displace affection for the dead person, this is known as identification with the dead and is accompanied by morbid dependency needs. The patient may imitate the dead person's mannerisms and speech. It is as though he is keeping the person alive within himself by this identification. He doesn't feel that he can find a person in reality who will do for him what the dead person did. The situation is complicated by the resentment he feels toward the dead person for leaving him or for not allowing him to grow up and think for himself. He is caught in a dependence dilemma. If he gets angry, he experiences the fear of losing love from the person with whom he is angry; so he turns in the hostility and anger at himself instead.

The reason that depressed people feel inferior, hopeless, and worthless is that they run themselves down and deny their capabilities. They think so little of themselves that they don't feel they are worth anyone's time or effort; so they cut themselves off from people and feel lonely, deserted, lost, and abandoned. Depressed Christians reflect this feeling of worthlessness. They feel they are of no use to God, they doubt their salvation, they dwell on the self-negating life, and they feed on any verse in the Bible that seems to tell them that they are no good, filthy, and inferior.

A few years ago I went to a church in the Midwest for a week of special meetings. The evening I arrived, I was met by a very friendly man in his forties. He greeted me with the admonition, "Preacher, really bear down hard on us, cut us to the core, tell us how bad we are. We really need to be revived." I thought to myself: "What a masochist this man must be. It sounds to me as though he needs just the oppostite. He needs to be built up in the faith and learn a little bit about self-acceptance."

During the week, I was invited to have dinner with him and his family. He decided that we should spend our time "redeeming the time"; so he turned it into a Bible study, exhorting me from passages he said were especially precious to him. Most of the verses had to do with man's depravity and there was a large sampling of all the judgment passages in the Bible. He found none of the promises and none of the passages on what God has done for man; everything was on hell and nothing was on heaven. The thing that troubled me throughout was that he seemed to be enjoying it. He found pleasure in running himself down.

This typifies the kind of person who has a deep hostility toward someone else. Unexpressed, this feeling is turned upon oneself. If the hate grows strong enough and one cannot discharge it toward the hated person, his self-hate may increase to the point of causing him to commit suicide. Suicide is not only a way to eliminate oneself, but it is also a way of punishing or destroying the hated person whose personality traits are a part of oneself. These depressives usually suffer from such physical problems as fatigue, poor sleep, and a reduced sex drive.

Causes of Depression

In addition to the loss of a loved object with its attendant deep feelings of hostility and dependency, excessive guilt is another cause of suffering for the depressive. He constantly needs approval. In his spiritual life he is always working to atone for his sins. But he never believes that he does enough, for his actions don't produce acceptance. The childhood of the depressive caused much of his problems. In the first year of life he may have felt that his mother loved him out of a sense of duty. Because of this feeling, he is impelled by a sense of duty to love his mother. Oftentimes the birth of a brother or sister will create depression in a youngster. The new arrival gets all the love and attention that he once had; so he tries feverishly to regain his mother's love by changing himself. He thinks he must be bad or his mother would continue to love him. He feels guilty and punishes himself for being so bad.

His experiences in later childhood may amplify these reactions. He is plagued by the fear of losing love. If his parents indicate that they love him when he is good but hate him when he is bad, he will decide that good behavior is conditional for love. Instead of feeling constant love and the understanding that good boys sometimes do naughty things, he associates lack of love with bad behavior.

Another cause of depression is inconsistency in parental standards. When discipline is inconsistent, it depends upon parental moods. What a parent considers bad one time is all right another time, and this leaves the child in doubt as to the proper guidelines of acceptable behavior. He may be taught both by his parents and his Sunday school teacher not to lie. But he sees his mother lie to the Fuller brush man and hears his father tell him to say to a phone caller, "Dad isn't home." This kind of parental inconsistency leaves the child bewildered and confused.

On the other hand, parental standards that are too high may contribute to feelings of depression. If the child is constantly harassed to be more nearly perfect than he is capable of being, he will naturally develop feelings of failure and futility.

Some parents force their children into unnatural roles of perfect behavior so that they, the parents, won't be embarrassed or so that they can take pride in their child. These roles often prevent the child from realizing his own worth as he feels he can never measure up to their expectations. An example of this would be the parents who expect excellent grades from an average child. If they berate the child for his average grades, his sense of self-esteem and his initiative may be damaged.

The Split Personality

Another category of emotional illness includes all those abnormalities from the withdrawn reactions of the *schizoid* personality to the more serious psychotic conditions known as *schizophrenia*. These conditions are not to be confused with the multiple personality described earlier. The schizoid personality handles his anxiety by detaching himself from people. He is afraid to become involved with people for fear they might hurt him. His life is characterized by escape from close personal relationships. His symptoms include aloofness, detachment, noninvolvement, and limited personal and social contacts. This type of person feels cut off, out of touch, and unreal. He has little interest in other people, their problems or their activities. If he attends social functions, he may talk freely but he has little real interest or emotional involvement with those around him. He may or may not manifest conscious anxiety. He limits his life experiences and feels inferior; so he turns to impersonal work, lives in a fantasy world of daydreams, and is more concerned with theories, ideas, and abstractions than with people. A schizoid person may find a real outlet for his fantasies by painting and other art work. He likes to escape to the hills, beaches, and mountains, where there is limited contact with other people.

His childhood usually reveals a home atmosphere of concealed unhappiness and tension, which is repressed by psychological insensitivity. There seems to have been unclear roles in his parents: there was no common understanding between them and no cooperation, mutual trust, or confidence. Instead, there was a sense of rivalry, belittling, threats of separation, and even solicitation of the child to take sides in supporting one parent's view. Usually, the parents are rejecting, anxious, ambivalent, and cold. Unless a child can count on a secure, trusting mother in the first year of life, and then relate to her later, he will always need to keep the world out of his life. He retreats from people because he fears that he might make excessive demands for their love and in this way lose them entirely.

If the person's withdrawn life continues without gratifying relationships with people or if his anxiety becomes too great, he may completely split from reality into the previously mentioned schizophrenic state. This is sometimes described by four words, all beginning with the letter *a*.

1. *Autism* — Complete withdrawal into the person's own world.

2. *Ambivalence* — Love and hate are so close together that the person cannot separate them. He cannot develop love for people because he hates them too much.

3. Disorders of *association* — His ego has cracked and his language becomes a "word salad," making no sense. He is unable to talk coherently. He cannot concentrate on one theme long enough to produce one thought.

4. Disorders of *affect* — What he says is not accompanied by the appropriate feeling tone. He may inappropriately start giggling or talk about serious things without any emotion.

Antisocial Behavior

The last areas of mental illness are the *character disorders*. These range from minor rebellion to the full-blown sociopathic personality. Sociopaths handle their anxiety and hostility by "acting out" in behavior the hostile feelings they have toward society. These people seem to have either a "constitutional" birth defect or a bad parental environment that keeps them from developing a strong, consistent superego. They are at odds with society or the status quo. Their condition is called a "character disorder" because they cannot maintain a consistently socially acceptable pattern of behavior for any length of time. They act impulsively, doing the thing they think of at the moment.

"Character" is defined as the permanent organization of a person's drives and the methods by which he achieves satisfaction for these drives. When we think of good character traits, we think of honesty, sincerity, and integrity. We refer to people as having a dependent character or an impulsive character. In the category of character disorders we find emotional instability and sex deviation, the latter including exhibitionism and homosexuality. Usually the alcoholic and the drug addict are also suffering from character disorders.

One of the most difficult and disheartening persons to deal with is the one afflicted with a character disorder. This kind of a person is described by the following example.

Mary had been divorced three times. She thought that before she married again she should come in for a checkup. She related a long history of up-and-down behavior. She had tried drugs, had been in trouble with the law, and had shoplifted. She described herself as an impulsive person, given to temper tantrums, and said she was the type of person who always followed the path of least resistance. When she wanted something, she

wanted it now and found it very difficult to delay any immediate
pleasureful aim for some future reward. She came for therapy
when she liked the previous session or had heard what she
wanted to hear. When she heard something she didn't like, she
simply did not show up for the next appointment. She felt no
sense of responsibility and if something went wrong, she would
call at any hour of the day or night and expect immediate
attention. When it seemed that I was making real progress with
her, she suddenly got involved in some discouraging problem
and repeated the process all over again. This is the typical
behavior of a person suffering from this emotional illness.

People with antisocial behavior reject authority and are irritating,
disappointing, and distressing to other people. At times they may
appear to be deeply involved with people emotionally, but this behavior is usually an act, and there is no depth to the relationship.
They do not make lasting friendships. They are like the Platte River—
a mile wide but only inches deep. Their main interest in other people
is to exploit them. They like to use people to gain their own ends.
Their judgment is usually poor. They are impulsive, irresponsible,
and self-centered to the exclusion of others. They seem to hear and
understand ethical values when they are presented to them, but they
find themselves unable and unwilling to live by these values. There
is a deep discrepancy between their level of intelligence and their
superego development.

In summary, the defenses of the ego in mental illness are the same
defenses as those used by normal people. It is the overuse of defenses
that makes a person pathological or abnormal. The depressive feels
the need to take in everything as his defense and to gobble up love
and affection. He is lost without approval from those around him.
The slightest amount of rejection may cause his whole world to
collapse. He also uses the defense of condensation, which means his
whole outlook is condensed into the mood he is in. So his mood
determines his outlook. If he feels bad, then everything appears to
be bad: the job is no good, the government is no good, the family
is no good — that is the way he sees things because he feels that he is
no good.

Have you ever noticed how impossible it is to talk a depressive out
of a depression? You may even attempt to show him how wonderful
things are. But you will not succeed, because he condenses everything
and sees everything in his world by the way he feels.

The schizoid personality, on the other hand, overuses the defense
of projection. He "physically" moves away from the world by "spitting
the world" out. He projects his inner tensions onto other people and
so withdraws from them. Whereas the mood determines the ideas in
the depressive (i.e., his attitudes about people and things), the

schizoid lets ideas determine mood. For instance, if he thinks it is Friday the 13th and if a black cat crosses his path, this combination of thought and event may produce within him the feeling of fear if he is superstitious. He also uses the defense of isolation. He feels that he doesn't need people; so he lives in a fantasy world by himself. The paranoid also uses the defense of projection, but it is usually more specific. He projects the way he feels onto other people and then feels that that is the way they feel about him. "I hate him" becomes "He hates me."

The person who has a character disorder is unable to use the defense so necessary to human development because he had a shallow relationship with significant persons in his life, such as his mother and father. He is unable to develop genuine, lasting, and positive relationships with people now; so he spends his life acting out his anxiety against society. In conversion reactions, the individual defends himself against undesirable unconscious thoughts mainly by overusing displacement and by distortion of hostility.

The obsessive-compulsive overuses the defense of elaboration and mastery. He talks on and on, elaborating facts in detail, without having any feelings about the things he is discussing. In his defense of mastery he falls in love with his ideas and his mind and attempts to outsmart people. He loves to win the argument.

In Part II we shall deal with some of the various methods of helping people who are troubled with these disorders. Special consideration will be given to the Christian.

PART II

What the Bible Teaches Us
About Ourselves

8

The Bible and the Hurt Ego

Applying Scripture to Specific Needs

MANY PEOPLE FEEL that merely reading the words from the Bible is a magical panacea for curing the problems, frustrations, and trials of everyday living.

Although the Bible confirms the spiritual nature of man, it is not an automatic cure-all without proper interpretation and application. The Bible suggests certain attitudes and behavior to help people grow toward perfection, but even Christ recognized that human frailty would interfere with man's striving to achieve goals.

Because man is an emotional creature, he tends to react to situations impulsively and immediately, rather than contemplatively. For example, it is a rare person who doesn't strike back in some way when struck. Good Christians lose their temper and self-control in frustrating situations. The old adage of counting to ten is wise but not always workable.

The analogy between the Bible and the field of medicine is well taken. There is no magic in medicine itself. Many different diseases have similar symptoms. It is only after careful analysis that an accurate diagnosis can be reached. The treatment of diabetes demands different medication from that required for the treatment of heart trouble, and the dosage will vary with the age and weight of the patient and the severity of the problem. Just as medicine encompasses a vast field of knowledge, so the Bible deals with many subjects and areas, too.

But there are many subjects the Bible does not deal with. And it may not exhaust all that is known about a subject it does speak about. Of course, when it speaks, it is infallible. Since its primary message concerns the salvation of mankind, it can meet the specific need of every person whose soul thirsts for a higher and holier knowledge of God and His will for one's life. There is a special passage for a person at a special time. And, if we are to be as wise as serpents and as harmless as doves (Matthew 10:16), we must apply biblical passages to our needs wisely.

The purpose of this chapter is not to discourage general Bible reading, but to introduce insight into using the Bible to meet specific needs. It should be apparent that many people cannot resolve their problems through Bible reading but must verbalize and share their problems with another human being.

I spoke to a middle-aged man at a seminar some time ago. He related to me the following experience.

> I had always been taught that all I ever needed in my spiritual experience was to take in the Word and obey it. I used to fly to Chicago and other places to the "deeper-life" conventions to get more answers. I don't mean to imply that I didn't get anything out of them but I found that I was getting more and more estranged from my true emotions. I was afraid to share what I really felt with other Christians because they might not think I was spiritual enough; so I found I was getting more and more isolated from people.
>
> Then I decided one day to become truly honest. I decided to share with a couple of friends the way I felt about things, to let them know what I was really like. If they hated me from that day on, that was their problem. I was going to risk it. As I shared, they shared. The more they shared, the more I shared. I realized, then, that the Christian life was a two-way street. When I shared myself, I got to know myself better, and when others accepted me as I was, I felt close to them and I was no longer isolated and alone. A strange thing happened. I not only felt closer to them but closer to God. My prayer life also improved and I became more honest in praying to my heavenly Father.

This man typically demonstrates the need we humans have for one another. Intercommunication on a deep level has no substitute in helping us resolve our problems.

God's Love Is Unconditional

With this background we proceed to correlate emotional problems with Scripture. Let's take the common problem of depression. The Christian who is depressed may feel that God is far away. He may doubt his salvation. Many *depressed Christians* seem to find passages in the Bible that augment their feelings of unworthiness. They dwell on verses about the failure of the flesh, the poison in the tongue, and the throat as an open sepulchre. They assume no man does good and that all men are altogether unprofitable. They also find verses of Scripture that feed their need of "shoulds and oughts." They dwell on literal interpretations of perfection and standards in the Christian life. They never feel they are "good enough"; so they need to continually examine their lives for some deep sin.

They may live righteous lives, yet they are always attempting to cleanse themselves. They describe the Spirit-filled life, but feel that they never attain it. They never enjoy anything they have. They have a constant battle to attain consecration, yieldedness, and victory, yet they can never define what these things really are in practical terms. They walk on a treadmill and never reach their goal.

They must first unlearn some things they had previously held as gospel truth. For example, one may feel that since he is saved, all his hostile resentment towards his brother should automatically be gone. When the hostility reappears after his spiritual honeymoon is over, he is smitten with guilt. It is like a voice saying, "You aren't really saved, or you wouldn't feel this way. You aren't spiritual." This guilt feeling may produce deep problems of tension and anxiety.

The first step in dealing with this problem from a biblical perspective would be to help the person understand that salvation does not automatically blot out memories and feelings from the past. Salvation is instantaneous. The saved man stands before God, immediately free from sin because of Christ's atoning blood. The process of growth, however, demands a "working through" or a dealing with these past feelings if they were repressed and are causing an emotional upheaval. Shoving them into the unconscious by trying to forget is harmful. The person needs to know that allowing his hostility to come to the surface will not jeopardize his relationship with God. God knows the thoughts and intents of the heart of man, and because He does, He sent His Son to die for the sins of the whole world. The person must express his hostility, confess it, and expose it. Then it becomes conscious and good ego-control results. Then the conflicts in his personality can disappear. More on this whole process will be discussed in Part III.

The second step is to help the person realize that *it is normal to have hateful feelings.* All men will respond with hostility when they are used, irritated, exploited, or cheated. Hostility or anger is a normal and universal human emotion. The person who never consciously feels any anger is emotionally ill.

The depressive also needs to understand that the Bible has many passages where open aggression is seen and hostility expressed.

Since depressives always seem to find in the Bible the verses that cause them to keep their hostile feelings in, we sometimes say to them, "You need to learn about the other half of the Bible." Then we explain that Jesus expressed many angry feelings. In Matthew 23:13-36, He called the scribes and Pharisees hypocrites. He pronounced woes on them. He likened them to whitewashed tombs and told them they were full of greed. Again, can you imagine the Savior having no angry emotion when He drove the money changers out of the temple in Jerusalem? (John 2:14-16). The record says He made a whip, drove them out, poured out their money, dumped over the tables, and gave them some stern, clear advice.

When a conflict arose over the use of the Sabbath, as recorded in Mark 3:1-5, we read of Jesus that "He looked around at them in anger." There are those who say He had a right to be angry but it was only righteous indignation. But it must be remembered that righteous indignation *is* anger and many of the things people do to us unjustly demand from us the same righteous indignation.

Again, in Romans 12:18 we have the admonition, "If it is possible, as far as it depends on you, live at peace with everyone." We thank God for the word "if." It just isn't possible to live peaceably with all men. Men in this world are too often unreasonable.

Then, in Ephesians 4:26 we find the command to be angry but not to sin. It is a good thing to tell a person about that aspect of his behavior that angers or irritates you, but it is another thing to throw dishes at him or smash his car or curse him. Being angry at a brother without cause is also quite another thing. The passage admonishes us, in addition, that we should not allow the sun to set on our wrath. We are to get it out in the open, then, by dealing with it through expression. If we allow it to go into the unconscious, it will produce many of the psychosomatic symptoms spoken about earlier.

Depressives, as a matter of fact, become that way because they do the very thing we advise against. They drive or turn their feelings within themselves rather than outward into the external world. The Christian life was never intended to be a passive, all-accepting type of life.

The depressive also needs to realize that God's love is unconditional, whereas his parent's love may have been conditional. These people need to dwell on the many comforting passages in the Scripture, such as Psalms 25, 27, 91, 121 and Matthew 6:25-34, which express God's great love. One other such passage is Psalm 34. Note some blessed verses in that Scripture: "O magnify the Lord with me. . . . I sought the Lord, and he answered me, and delivered me from all my fears. . . . This poor man cried, and the Lord heard him, and saved him out of all his troubles. The angel of the Lord encamps around those who fear him, and delivers them. O taste and see that the Lord is good! Happy is the man who takes refuge in him! . . . Those who seek the Lord lack no good thing. . . . Many are the afflictions of the righteous; but the Lord delivers him out of them all. . . . The Lord redeems the life of his servants; none of those who take refuge in him will be condemned" (Psalm 34:3, 4, 6, 7, 8, 10, 19, 22).

We Must Express Our Feelings

The *obsessive-compulsive* has some of the same features of the depressive in that he is defending himself against deep hostility and is plagued with guilt. Even doing a pleasurable thing may create guilt and the need to atone. It becomes a constant struggle of deciding, "Should I do it or shouldn't I?" Unlike the depressive, the obsessive lives in a world of head knowledge. He thinks and thinks and thinks some more. The problem is that he does not feel or experience things. He reads avidly. His intellectual faculties become supreme.

I remember when I was training for Christian service many years ago at the Moody Bible Institute in Chicago, two fellow students seemed to be terribly concerned about the rightness or the wrongness of certain biblical truths. They argued by the hour on such things as infant baptism, believers' baptism by immersion, predestination, and eternal security.

I often wondered if they ever got anything settled in their discussions. To me it seemed that their discussions were endless. Later it came to me that what I was witnessing was nothing more than two obsessive individuals who were not really interested in solving any Bible doctrine but were getting their satisfaction in the arguments themselves.

There are among Christians many obsessives who like to argue these doctrines.

In helping the obsessive with the Bible, we must remember that feeding him new facts generally will only feed his thirst for "knowledge." The goal here should be to have him express his feelings about certain passages. Since this kind of person likes to argue Scripture, one of the main things would be to avoid the pro and con arguments of certain Bible doctrines.

The need to argue seems more important to this person than the meaning of the passage itself. It might be helpful to show him how he tries to conform outwardly while hiding some objectionable feelings about his own inadequacy and hostility from himself and others. Devotional passages that encourage him to feel God's presence should be read regularly, rather than doctrinal passages dealing with controversial matters. An example is Psalm 27:1, 4, 11, 13, 14: "The Lord is my light and my salvation; whom shall I fear? The Lord is the stronghold of my life; of whom shall I be afraid? . . . One thing have I asked of the Lord, that will I seek after; that I may dwell in the house of the Lord all the days of my life, to behold the beauty of the Lord, and to inquire in his temple. . . . Teach me thy way, O Lord, and lead me on a level path. . . . I believe that I shall see the goodness of the Lord in the land of the living! Wait for the Lord; be strong and let your heart take courage; yea, wait for the Lord!"

He Can Trust God

The Bible tells us that "all Scripture is God-breathed and is useful for teaching, rebuking, correcting, and training in righteousness" (2 Timothy 3:16). It also tells us that God has given us a sound mind (2 Timothy 1:7). It is very important that we have discernment to know who needs what Scripture verse at a particular given period of time. This fact is vital when dealing with the *paranoid* personality who feels that everybody is out to get him, talking about him, or trying to control his thoughts.

Do not show him such passages as these: "The word of God . . . judges the thoughts and attitudes of the heart" (Hebrews 4:12). "The eyes of the Lord are in every place, keeping watch on the evil and the good" (Proverbs 15:3). "You will be betrayed by parents, brothers, relatives and friends, and they will put some of you to death. All men will hate you because of me" (Luke 21:16, 17). "Be always on the watch, and pray that you may be able to escape all that is about to happen, and that you may be able to stand before the Son of Man" (Luke 21:36).

The *paranoid*, who finds it difficult to trust people, should be encouraged to study passages dealing with the loving nature of God. Romans 8:14-17, for example, expresses the loving relationship God establishes with His children: "Those who are led by the Spirit of God are sons of God. For you did not receive a spirit that makes you a slave again to fear, but you received the Spirit who makes you sons. And by him we cry, 'Abba, Father.' The Spirit himself testifies with our spirit that we are God's children. Now if we are children, then we are heirs — heirs of God and co-heirs with Christ, if indeed we share in his sufferings in order that we may also share in his glory."

If a paranoid can somehow feel that God will not harm him, his anxiety can possibly be reduced, and this new relationship might grow and be used to develop a more trusting relationship with people. Passages that refer to God's knowing our thoughts and the intents of our hearts may feed the person's paranoia and should be avoided.

The Need for Acceptance

People who are *neurotic* or *insecure* need a strong scriptural diet of positive verses that strengthen their relationship with God and man. They do not do well with verses that threaten them, make them feel cut off from God, or make them feel that they need to live up to an illusionary high standard.

They need verses that make them feel accepted as they are — Scriptures that show them a caring God who is interested in them as individuals. The book of Psalms is especially good. Other passages not previously mentioned are Psalms 23; 37:3-7; and 107:20-30. There are also many other parts of Scripture that may especially help these people: Isaiah 40:28-31; Jeremiah 33:3; Matthew 6:25-34; Romans 8:38, 39; 1 Corinthians 10:13; and others.

The *schizophrenic* also, with his tendency to withdraw, needs to experience life in a loving, accepting way. Being close to people has only brought problems to him in the past, so he has cut off his capacity to feel. He says, "If you don't feel, then you can't experience painful emotions." He needs to find passages about the grace of God and His love and His concern, and he needs to communicate his feelings about these passages with others. The human interchange is a very important ingredient in helping him. But one should not try to get too close, because of the anxiety this relationship might create.

Bible Restraints Required

The *sociopathic* person, who acts out his anxiety against authority and convention, lacks inner control. This is notably the one person who needs to feel very much his accountability to God. He needs to be squarely faced with the plan of salvation and the fundamental laws of God concerning man's behavior, such as we find in the Sermon on the Mount (Matthew 5-7). He must make the spiritual value system taught in the Bible his own.

People who are sociopathic seem to have an unusually poor conscience and a warped sense of right and wrong. Their wrongful behavior needs to be pointed out to them in a firm manner. In a relationship with another human being, they must learn to control certain activities in order to maintain a lasting and positive relationship with God and man. Some of these people have responded favorably to strong confrontation and have expressed the feeling that someone cared enough to seek and to restrain their behavior.

God Understands

In the *anxiety-laden, hysterical personality*, we must find out why the person is so anxious. Is it a sense of guilt and the fear of punishment that is creating the anxiety? If the hysteric is feeling guilty because of an immoral past, he should be shown passages dealing with the unconditional forgiveness of God and the kindness and acceptance that Jesus offered people who had this same problem. John 8:1-12, which deals with the woman caught in adultery, is the best.

If a person's anxiety is caused by personality immaturity, which is being threatened by adult responsibility, passages on the leading, guiding, and sustaining hand of God should be shown him. If tension is caused by secret, sinful wishes over which the person seems to have no control, then the patient should be helped by exploring and dealing with these wishes, being assured that God will give him the strength to face himself and will not condemn him for such thoughts.

In summary, it is important to discern exactly what the problem is and then apply the appropriate Scriptures directly to it. It is vital to realize that the person *needs* to talk his problem out so the problem areas can come to the surface. A short, well-chosen verse at the proper time is worth chapters of Scripture quoted randomly or indiscriminately.

9

What the Bible Teaches About the Self

Must the Ego Be Eliminated?

ONE OF THE ways the believer can be helped to escape the disorders cited in the preceding chapter is to have a correct understanding, at least, of the scriptural view of the self and how to deal with oneself. As previously noted, quite a number of Christians are convinced that the "ego" must be eliminated because of certain Bible references. Let's examine the verses that are commonly held to support this point of view. The first is Galatians 2:20: "I have been crucified with Christ and I no longer live, but Christ lives in me. The life I live in the body I live by faith in the Son of God, who loved me and gave himself for me."

What does this verse really say? Who was crucified? The meaning of this verse seems clear and simple. If we take this verse literally, we must assume that we should die on the cross with Christ. This is, of course, impossible. To the contrary, the primary emphasis is on living for Christ. Through personal faith in Christ's atoning death we have been identified with His death. But as we continue to live this life in the flesh, the "I" still lives in the body. Paul twice states, "I live." The crucified life means the wall of isolation separating us from God, which was present before salvation, is broken so we can truly live! There is fellowship, strength, and communion with the divine "I" through Jesus Christ. There is a sharing of the divine and the human wills made possible through the justification and atonement of Jesus Christ. This verse, then, provides no basis for the teaching that our egos are to be negated.

Closely related to this verse is Luke 9:23-25: "If anyone would come after me, he must deny himself and take up his cross daily and follow me. For whoever wants to save his life will lose it, but whoever loses his life for me will save it. What good is it for a man to gain the whole world, and yet lose or forfeit his very self?"

It's a Matter of the Will

Notice that the man is to take up "his cross." A man can't face the problems of life if he doesn't have a strong ego. Christ is saying, "I have a will for your redeemed human ego. Your ego can develop properly only in my will." The losing of the self is actually a dependence upon our heavenly Father, as described in the vine/branch analogy (John 15). Christ actually saves or strengthens the self and allows it to grow and develop properly.

From a doctrinal point of view, the passage is pointing forward to Christ's death. Jesus is asking His disciples about their willingness to identify with Him as He is about to suffer and die for the sins of the whole world. To many around Him, He was popular. Tens of thousands turned out to hear Him. Even His enemies said, "No one ever spoke the way this man does" (John 11:46).

Were they simply following a fad? Christ was trying to give them insight in order to make them willing to die for His name rather than to deny their faith. We feel strongly that this passage is not offering a premium to the person who lives a life of suffering. God never intended that we have self-hate to the extent that we destroy ourselves. What He asks is that we follow His Son and not deny our faith. If we must suffer because we believe in Him, then suffering is justified. He asks us to live for Him, and this may involve being persecuted for our faith.

Breaking With Past Life

Luke 9:23ff. seems to be clearly teaching two things: first, salvation, and second, discipleship. When a man comes to Christ, he first must make up his mind about the cost. He must make a clear-cut decision. When he denies himself, salvation is seen in a different dimension. He does not expect things to go right simply as part of a gift of being a Christian. Rather, he is willing to live for Christ whether things in the world go right or wrong.

Then he is to take up his cross as a symbol of breaking with his past life where all his emotional attachments were with the world. This, indeed, requires a new, deep loyalty.

This passage in no way can be construed to mean that we are to get rid of ourselves, since the very next verse reminds us that we will *find* ourselves when we first *lose* ourselves. If we find ourselves, then we truly exist. We lose ourselves when we live only for ourselves. As one man put it, "Everywhere I go I spoil everything. I want to get myself off my back and out from under my feet. I'm tripping all over myself all the time." It is in the losing of myself that I find myself and a wider life.

Learning to "Lose" Myself

In the early days of my psychological practice, I experienced the value of losing myself. What I discovered illustrates well this "losing and finding" principle.

My schedule was full of people wanting to get an appointment with me. Inside I was afraid to refer any of them to other psychologists for fear that if my load fell off I would be short of clients. In the meantime I was killing myself physically and emotionally, enjoying little in life because of the severe work load.

I eventually made the decision, with the Lord's help, to lighten the load by referring people to others. And, in losing myself in this way, I multiplied my ministry. As a matter of fact, to my amazement I was never short of clients and the counseling Center is growing. I now have a staff of eight men and a secretary and it looks as though we will be enlarging our staff considerably in the future. In this way I am reaching many more than I could have by myself. Also, the expansion has provided greater opportunity for teaching and learning business management and procedures.

These things bring me a greater sense of achievement and fulfillment than I could ever have had by working alone. The fellowship with others, too, is uplifting in this specialized Christian ministry. All this, because I became willing to "lose" self by referring clients elsewhere. Only then did I "find" myself and an exciting, fulfilling life!

Surrender to a Higher Good

The biggest problem that we all face is the constant problem of surrender. Yet this, seen and experienced in the proper perspective, is the key to real happiness.

Dr. E. Stanley Jones once spoke in Glendale, California, on the subject of the meaning of seeking first the kingdom of God. His five points are very helpful: (1) There is first a stage of indecision when it comes to surrender. (2) Then comes the stage of making up one's mind. (3) The stage of giving up self so that one belongs to that other person follows. (4) Then comes the stage of daring to unite with God with a mutual will and service. (5) The final stage results in mutual adjustment, mind to mind, will to will, in a daily relationship through the years. This is true of marriage. It is also true of the Christian life.

There is another way to illustrate the principle of "losing" and "finding" oneself. One of the typical things in marriage counseling that we meet every day is the triangle love affair. It may start this way: after so many years of marriage, the marriage gets dull and drab and the man finds the pretty young secretary down the hall to be much more beautiful and more willing to listen to him. She seems more intelligent, is up on world events, and has more education.

Her office is close and she can be seen every day for lunch and snack times. He begins to confide in her his feelings of loneliness and his problems. She says just the right things. She needs a strong man to look up to. He meets this need and so the relationship deepens. He discovers, eventually, that he has fallen in love! He may even believe that he is experiencing love for the very first time. He suddenly finds himself torn. He wants to go with her, but he is a Christian and she is not. Then there is the problem of the children. "If I go with her, what will this do to the children and what will all my Christian friends think?"

He finally makes the decision to break it up, contrary to all his emotional feelings, and to experience "death" or loss of someone very important in order to go back to a wife that he may respect, but for whom he has no feelings.

Besides, he recognizes that he is caught in a jam, knowing that he cannot financially support two families. So he stays at home with all the conveniences and enjoys the children, but he has no feelings for his wife. He has everything, yet he is miserable. Everywhere he and his wife go, he sees the cafe or music center where he and the secretary enjoyed pleasant, romantic moments. The conflict makes him wonder if he made a mistake by going home to his wife. Will he ever have any feelings for her again? How can he get the other woman out of his thoughts?

Only One Alternative

In all our years of counseling and facing this dilemma with many people, we have found only one solution. A person in this situation must make an irrevocable decision and reckon the third party dead. The man, for instance, must tell the woman that everything is finished. He must never call her, dine with her, or write to her again. She must become "dead" to him and he must experience the accompanying mourning process. It is only after a decisive act of the will that reckons himself "dead" to her that things become straightened out. Then another deliberate act of the will must follow. He must will to love his wife. He cannot serve two masters. To simply wait at home and hope that feelings will once again reappear for his wife and that feelings for the other woman will automatically disappear does not work!

The human ego alone will never relinquish a relationship with a person, since it follows the path of least resistance. It takes a deliberate act of the will to break off a relationship. It is only at this point that feelings for the wife will again appear.

So it is with marriage. And so it is with the Christian life concerning salvation and discipleship. He that denies and loses himself for a higher good and purpose will *find* himself and happiness in the kingdom of God!

What About the Last Days?

Another text often used to support the view that self should be repudiated is 2 Timothy 3:2: "People will be lovers of themselves." This is presented as one of the bad aspects or characteristics of the perverted human condition in the last days of this church age. Certain Christians have proclaimed this verse as proof that self-love is corrupt.

But when we look at the verse in its wider and proper context, a different meaning is intended. The apostle Paul makes self-love, in this case, synonymous with selfishness. This meaning of self-love is the total concern for self without any feelings for the other person. It is the gratification of desire without thought for the other person. Where there is no empathy and love for others, the result is covetousness, boasting, truce breaking, false accusation, and total sensual self-satisfaction.

Self-Love Is Essential

The Bible actually teaches that there is a self-love that is healthy. A healthy self-love is an acceptance of the talents God has given one and confidence in those abilities and the achievements that result from the use of them. Self-love is healthy when there is an equal love for others. Matthew 22:39 states, "Love your neighbor as *yourself*" (italics mine). If I don't love and respect myself, how can I respect and relate to someone else? There can be no giving of charity and love to another person if I don't think I am worthy of such actions. To force myself to live in squalid poverty so that I can give all to missions is not giving proper attention to myself. To keep all for myself and give none to others is equally wrong. There is a delicate balance here between loving one's neighbor and loving oneself and one should not overlook the correct interpretation to preserve that balance. Indeed, there is a biblical self-acceptance.

Healthy self-love and self-esteem is also seen in Matthew 6:26: "Look at the birds of the air; they do not sow or reap or store away in barns, and yet your heavenly Father feeds them. Are you not much more valuable than they?" Jesus states emphatically that God loves and protects the animals in nature that have no talents and can be witnesses to His creation only by their existence. But notice that Jesus asks, "Are you not much more valuable than they?" It is our human ego and sense of personal identity and worth that distinguish us from the lower animals and enable us to love and relate to God. Only man is capable of loving and worshiping the Creator.

The equality of the "me" and "thee" is again taught in the marriage relationship in Ephesians 5:28: "In the same way, men ought to love their wives as their *own* bodies. He who loves his wife loves himself" (italics mine). Without a sound concept of self and a realistic love of self, the individual is limited in his ability to love God, his mate, his neighbor, and his enemy — all of which God has commanded man to do.

Examples of a Strong Ego

The healthy ego is exemplified in the life of the apostle Paul, who said in Philippians 4:13: "I can do everything through him who gives me strength." Paul had to face the realities of life: earning a living, reasoning with unreasonable men, and facing dangerous opposition in distant lands. He did these things with the help of Christ the divine "Ego," who gave him purpose, direction, and courage to face the rigors of life.

Another example of Paul's healthy ego is found in his statements in 2 Timothy 4:7: "I have fought a good fight, I have finished my course, I have kept the faith." Many might accuse Paul of gross egotism and bragging, but he *did* fight a good fight, he *did* finish his course, and he *did* keep the faith — which made him justifiably "proud."

If we underestimate our talents to prove our humility, we do God a disservice. Realistically appraising our talents and accomplishments is consistent with the divine command.

Self-Castigation Often Reveals a Weak Ego

Frequently, when a pastor comes to a new church, he receives a request for judgmental preaching: "We want to hear how bad we are. Really shake us up." When this request is realistically examined, it is sometimes seen to represent an unresolved guilt complex. Yet the very people who think they need this type of preaching are often regular in their church attendance, spiritually concerned, and active in church affairs and duties. Why then do they feel the need to be castigated as wicked sinners? This kind of religious fervor is really defeating them rather than strengthening them. In essence, this type of person is hoping the pastor will hammer him into the ground or expose some sin that he hasn't faced.

Such a person has a need to be punished. But his sense of relief under preaching of this kind is only temporary because he has an overall bad concept of himself that no amount of judgmental preaching can dispel. Instead of accepting the forgiveness that God has provided mankind through the ultimate sacrifice of His Son,

Jesus Christ, on the cross, he is still searching his heart for evil. This is a far cry from a healthy relationship with the Lord. Compulsive worship is slavery; spontaneous worship is sublime.

What about the person who repeatedly comes to the altar or seeks out the pastor concerning his salvation? The pastor may counsel him over and over again with prayer and Scripture, but this person may still have doubts. If a so-called spiritual problem does not clear up with spiritual means, we must accept the fact that it is not a spiritual problem but a psychological one.

In this case, the man may be suffering from a weak ego and depression. He may feel alienated from people. He cannot get close to anyone. He has shut off his emotions so that he will not be hurt. He has built up a wall of isolation between himself, his fellowman, and God that can't be broken down by simply reading the Bible. If he is incapable of loving himself, he is incapable of loving others and is consequently insecure, frightened, and defensive.

1 John 4:20 tells us, "Anyone who does not love his brother, whom he has seen, cannot love God, whom he has not seen." We know our parents before we know God. If parental conflicts, such as rejection, have caused us to withdraw from sound relationships with other people, how shall we be able to love God, whom we have not seen? If the self-rejection is too severe, the person might have to receive some corrective acceptance from another loving human being before he will be able to feel God's loving grace. The Sunday school slogan states this idea well: "First Johnny gets to know his teacher, and then he discovers his teacher's God."

Distorting Bible Truth

We must understand how vital it is "to rightly divide the Word of truth" (2 Timothy 2:15). When a man concludes that the victorious Christian life and discipleship require a weak ego, he is really turning on himself in self-hate and, therefore, distorts biblical truth. To justify his attitude of self-hate, a man may quote Luke 14:26: "If anyone comes to me and does not hate his father and mother, his wife and children, his brothers and sisters — yes, even his own life — he cannot be my disciple."

To take this passage literally is to pervert the Scriptures and distort the true meaning of Christian love and charity. Jesus is employing a common Hebraic literary device for emphatic comparison. The passage is saying that our love for Christ must be so strong that human love appears to be hate by comparison. It is like holding up a shirt that appears white until it is compared with a dazzling new white shirt.

Unfortunately, Christians have held fallacious views for years because they have taken these verses out of context, have ignorantly

misapplied them, or have blindly followed erroneous traditional interpretations without seriously studying them for their true teaching
and meaning.

We have seen that the vital, vigorous, victorious, Christian life
cannot be experienced unless we have a good concept of ourselves.
True, we should give the credit for our talents to God, but we must
not dissipate or waste those talents because we think ourselves
unworthy of them.

A closer scrutiny of the so-called negative, "self-hate" verses in the
Bible reveals that they are not at all against one's having a good,
strong self-concept. A person with a good ego, then, is not all for
self nor all for others, but he loves others as he loves himself. He
has the ability to share. A good ego is absolutely necessary for one to
have a good relationship with God.

10

Let's Take a Look at Pride

Is It Right to Deflate Your Ego?

ONE OF THE great fears among Christians about the subject of self is that looking too favorably upon oneself will lead to pride, rebellion, and maybe to a final state of not sensing a need of God at all anymore. They feel they must constantly downgrade themselves and remind themselves that "nothing good" lives in their "sinful nature" (Romans 7:18). As a result, they lead a rigid, austere, narrow life. Instead of accepting their feelings of self-worth, they constantly deny themselves and don't get involved in anything they think might lead them astray.

Their reasoning is faulty. Examples of such reasoning are these: "I should not eat because eating may lead to gluttony." "I should not enjoy a hobby because it may become an idol." "I must not accept my sexuality and my natural response toward a member of the opposite sex because it may lead to adultery."

By constant rituals, under the guise of spiritual dedication, they only isolate themselves further from finding their real selves. They live compulsively instead of spontaneously. They never really know their true feelings. They are enslaved to the "tyranny of the should" instead of finding out *who they really are*. They have become, as the saying goes, "so heavenly-minded they are of no earthly good." We might better state it this way: "They use their false spirituality as a defense against coming to terms with their God-given humanity." They forget that men in this life never will become "angels" and that the Lord expects all to accept their humanity and develop it for His glory.

Healthy Pride

Most of man's fears about accepting himself, his personality, and his talents center around the fact that the Christian does not want to be filled with pride. To be sure, the Bible states, "The proud one shall stumble and fall, with none to raise him up" (Jeremiah 50:32).

85

"God opposes the proud, but gives grace unto the humble" (James 4:6). "So, if you think you are standing firm, be careful that you don't fall" (1 Corinthians 10:12). We point out, however, that to say that every form of pride is evil or bad is not the truth either. There is such a thing as healthy pride or self-esteem based on substantial attributes.

When we moved to La Habra, California, we were plagued by too much sun coming through the windows on the south side of the house. I considered putting up awnings over all the windows but decided that would look tacky and, because there were so many windows, it seemed impractical. The only real solution I could find was to put on a complete aluminum patio cover, shading the whole area.

I decided to try it myself after carefully studying the project. I bought the unit, complete with decorator posts. There was a real difficulty involved in attaching the cover to the wall of the house and still getting it under the deep, overhanging roof. This also required leaving just the right angle on the cover for drainage and yet placing it high enough so we would be able to see out of the windows without blockage. When I put it up, it just cleared on the top side by one quarter of an inch and had just enough slope for proper drainage. When completed, it looked beautiful — just like a professional job. Whenever I think about it, I have a justifiable sense of pride in this achievement.

A soldier may take justifiable pride in the fact that in risking his life he saved several of his buddies from an agonizing death. Parents may take pride in the fact that their son became the valedictorian of the graduating class. Healthy pride certainly encourages a person and motivates him to achieve. It is healthy for a man to draw upon his own resources and gifts in order to appraise his assets and liabilities and to cultivate good human relationships. We might look at this kind of pride as an accurate appraisal of oneself, or a feeling of self-confidence.

False Pride

The Bible often condemns pride as evil and says that the proud person, therefore, will fall. What kind of pride is this? This kind of pride is false because it is a distortion of truth. It is any defense used against looking at one's true self and relating to people as equals. It is a neurotic state.

What is shocking for most people to realize is that the cocky, smug, overconfident person is underneath actually weak and unsure of himself and is trying to live up to an idealized image of what he feels he should be. His life is a sham. He never really knows himself or allows others to know him. He becomes alienated from himself and divided against himself. He must always defend himself from seeing what he really is. He runs after prestigious values, spending his best energies to protect himself from being found out. He is unrelated to the group personally but uses the group for personal prestige. He never feels a part of it or a sense of belonging to it.

Defenses Against One's Self

We now look at the various ways in which the neurotically proud person defends himself against looking at his real self and furthers his "idealized" image. Perhaps you have known a person who has great talent and ability. When his accomplishments or potentialities are pointed out, he simply shrugs his shoulders and allows the compliment to run off like water from a duck's back. Such a person finds it difficult to accept his musical talent, his artistic ability, or even the fact that he is intelligent. He does not know how to accept a compliment. That person does not want to look at his real self and is proud of the fact that he is not being himself.

There is also the person who is anxious to preserve his illusions about being a saint, a mastermind, or a creative genius. He cannot bear the thought that anyone would question the "idealized" image of himself. He prides himself on being an individualist and cannot accept suggestions from others on his need for change.

Another manifestation of this pride is found in the person who is proud of his power to manipulate. He knows how to get something for nothing, cheat people out of money, and keep others confused or controlled. He is insulted if advice that he gives is not immediately followed. He is proud that he can keep people at a distance while they are working for him.

There is also the proud person who cannot ask for help from anyone even though it is desperately needed. He cannot accept clothes for his children, food for his table, or transportation for his family to church. He is too proud to admit that he is down or that he is that poor. He hides behind the cloak that he doesn't want to take advantage of anyone. He may even appear very spiritual in his refusal. It is intended to impress the possible donor with his humility but, in reality, to accept help is too hurtful to his pride, since it is admitting that he is not all his "idealized" image says he should be.

Another manifestation of this is the "holy Joe." He has such high moral standards that he is proud of his holiness. He appears to be rather godlike. In preaching to others, he maintains his omnipotence and passes on to others the standards of his "idealized" image, which he himself would like to live up to but can't. When caught while not living up to his own standard, he always knows how to turn this into his own advantage.

If he is accused of being rude, he turns it into "firmness" or "honesty" for the good of the other person. He is always able to twist things. He can convert legalism into "righteousness," or judgment of his brother into "spiritual concern." *All flaws become premeditated spiritual virtues.* He uses his imagination to turn his faults into gems of which he can be proud. A prejudice becomes a "spiritual conviction." A dependent need for another person is turned into "loving concern." Inconsistency is called the "freedom of the believer under grace."

This type of person prides himself in not being vulnerable. Yet at the same time he is very vulnerable. He collapses at the slightest rebuff because he has not developed a strong self-image. When he is challenged, there are no resources of a real self upon which to draw. At this point he may withdraw from any situation that might produce further rejection or hurt, or he might project his feelings by saying that these poor people just don't understand him. He may even become quite self-righteous and try to boost his image by telling himself he is big enough to overlook such petty statements.

Paradoxes in Behavior

If he withdraws, he will stay away from any situation that might cause embarrassment, such as taking courses where he might get something less than an A. He won't make a sales pitch before other salesmen because he may make a mistake. He may even refrain from asking a girl for a date because he would be humiliated if he were turned down. He may never ask for a raise in wages or apply for a scholarship, since anything short of immediate and complete success tends to distort his grandiose image of himself and what he should be. These patterns lead to paradoxes in his behavior.

Since he cannot live up to his "idealization," he even gets severe with himself and may become very masochistic and vindictive toward himself. This is the basis for many guilt complexes — not being able to live up to one's own "ideal" of himself. Hostility at this point toward others may become very pronounced, since he desperately needs to see his wounded pride restored.

He may even withdraw completely from people and situations where his pride has been hurt. He may relinquish his interest in sports, politics, or his field of specialty because he is not doing a perfect job. He cannot share. He must be the most gifted one in the class or he may quit under the guise that it is a field in which he is no longer interested or that the teacher is not good and he didn't want to waste valuable time in such a course. Since people don't love him, he beats them to the punch by deciding not to love them first. In this way he bolsters his pride system. If he offends a friend, it is because he didn't have time to give him what he needed. If someone is hurt by his words, he rationalizes that his intentions were good. Gradually, he may even move into a complete fantasy world. He may even discuss his problem as though he were talking about some third person in the room. He makes a sharp distinction between himself and his neurosis. He gears himself in his system of avoidances to stop all future disappointments.

The tragedy in the neurotic pride system is that this person dies on the vine and never finds himself or develops his true feeling so that he can grow. The neurotically proud person finds it safer not to try than to try and fail. His fantasy becomes greater and greater and his illusion grows. He could have been president if he had tried. He could have become another Picasso if he had wanted to, or a Beethoven if he had applied himself.

Two Kinds of Pride

We can see, then, that there are two types of pride. One is a healthy self-respect and the other, an illusionary, false, fantasy style of life. The latter seems to fit very accurately the type of pride abhorred in the Scriptures, the kind that can burst so easily.

In our culture the word "pride" has seemingly been used almost exclusively in a derogatory sense and illustrates only the second kind of pride used above. In no way are we to construe that healthy self-respect is more than a humble Christian spirit with a healthy attitude towards one's talents, abilities, and world. Humility is the recognition of the limitations and real abilities one possesses. It keeps things in perspective. It is still a great virtue. "Humble yourselves before the Lord, and he will lift you up" (James 4:10).

Since Christ is the Way, the Truth, and the Life, He wants us to deal with reality. The neurotically proud person needs our understanding. In most cases, he gained little self-confidence in childhood. The help he needed from his parents in the building of his self-image was severely restricted. He needed warmth; a feeling of belonging, confidence, and care; and a consistent frame of reference — all of which he never received.

To scold, condemn, and point out the proud neurotic's faults will only tend to isolate him even more from God's people and make it impossible for him to find himself. He probably never felt needed and wanted for himself but only for the neurotic needs of parents who used him to satisfy their own deficiencies or prestige.

11

Christianity Is a Balanced Life

A Look at Reality

As a MAN matures in his Christian experience, he becomes more and more perceptive of reality because of his past experience. But since reality testing is always in a state of flux because people, situations, and conditions change, he should recognize that his ego must continually adjust to changing events at any given moment if he is to develop and mature.

Just as the experienced machinist will produce more accurate work than the apprentice because of his experience, so the experienced ego will be better able to adjust, adapt, and amend itself to the situation at hand because of previous experience, trial, and error.

For example, two Christians may believe identical doctrines in the Bible, but while one may hold a healthy, vibrant faith because of a particular doctrine, the other may become upset and even ill because the doctrine increases his neurotic condition. The difference is the result of the way the doctrine is applied or in the degree the person is able to assimilate its meaning.

Beyond Explanation

A typical illustration will help us to comprehend this phenomenon. John was led to Christ by one of the fellows at work. His conversion was dramatic. He had been drifting through life with a tremendous guilt complex. Life held no purpose or meaning for him and he constantly found himself in a state of anxiety. He was troubled about world conditions, race riots, the high cost of living, the tremendously competitive dog-eat-dog economy, and the seeming indifference of society to his personal plight.

Then one day he discovered a deeper sense of inner peace and outer purpose. His feelings of anxiety about himself and his relation to this world disappeared. A new, true meaning for living entered his spirit. The contrast that he felt between his old way of life with its frustrations and purposelessness and his new-found life with its abundance of joy and deep meaning was beyond explanation. John begins to wonder why the whole world hasn't come to Christ. He realizes that Christ is truly the Way, the Truth, and the Life, and so he now wants to convert everyone with whom he comes in contact. He is challenged by the slogan, "It is better to burn out for God than to rust out for the devil." He distributes tracts, contributes to the missionary program, and teaches a Sunday school class. He feels that if he does not warn the wicked of their ways, their blood will be on his hands.

He has developed a strict concern for what is right and wrong. He has a list of dos and don'ts by which he measures everyone else's spiritual life. He becomes a crusader for truth. He studies the minute doctrines of the Bible. He is concerned with the right method of baptism — whether infant sprinkling, pouring, or immersion is the correct procedure.

He spends a lot of time sifting through the passages about the eternal security of the believer. He deliberates on Calvinism or Arminianism, a covenant theology or a dispensational theology, which church is closest to the New Testament church, and whether Christ will come before or after the tribulation.

But this intense interest in discovering the truth leaves him insensitive to people, their problems, needs, and feelings. Other people's indifference to his zeal leaves him with the impression that the world doesn't seem to care. Because these people don't share his views, he is shocked that they could turn down the Savior who has done so much for him. He knows they need Christ, and yet they are unmoved by his testimony.

Since the unsaved reject him, he moves closer to the church people for fellowship. He volunteers to be chairman of the Christmas program. He works very hard for a successful program. In fact, he puts his whole heart and soul into this project, but it isn't quite right. He is criticized by some of the church membership who suggest changes or improvements. He is crushed. He feels that he is never thanked for his efforts, only criticized for his failures.

"Christianity Won't Work"

About this time John discovers that his best friend, Sam, the man who first led him to Christ, is getting a divorce. He is horribly shocked and disillusioned. He even begins to doubt the reality of his conversion because his spiritual idol has fallen. He begins to experience doubt in his prayer life, even though he has been zealously guarding his devotions. It seemed at first that God wrought miracles in answer to his prayers, but now so many of them seem to be unanswered. He doesn't feel there is really any point in prayer. "Prayers are fantasies.

The miraculous finger of God is really just fate or coincidence," he reasons. "Whatever befell me would have happened anyway, regardless of prayer."

His whole religious life is suddenly filled with doubts: the existence of God, the inspiration of the Scriptures, his faith in other Christians. He is angry with his Christian friends and God. But these feelings make him feel more guilty than ever. He is now caught in a double bind. He reasons that Christians shouldn't feel this way, but he does, and so he feels guilty about it. Yet if he holds in his hostility and doesn't express the way he feels, he becomes mentally depressed, too.

He now begins to experience severe headaches, feels withdrawn, and is depressed. He feels that he may have to choose between being a good Christian and being emotionally healthy. His legalistic teachings seem to be perfectionistic to the point where they isolate him from himself and other people.

He finally concludes, "In order to cope with life I must relinquish my religion. God really helps only those who help themselves." He feels that waiting on God now becomes nothing but a crippling mechanism that has kept him from interacting with his world. He feels that he must do anything that needs to be done, that there is no use depending on God. He becomes a pragmatist; i.e., he has the philosophy that says, "If it works, it is right."

In order to preserve some semblance of faith, he starts searching for a more liberal church. At last he is freed from his legalism. He feels free to swear, drink, and smoke. He not only stops attending church but he also criticizes or belittles the "poor fools who are bound to the ritual of church attendance." He now feels completely free.

"You Only Live Once"

John has now reached the point where he feels unshackled and liberated from his former beliefs. He knows that time is running out and if he is going to prove himself, he has to do it alone. He decides to enroll in college and become a physicist. This will boost his ego and increase his chances of getting in on the really big money. He thinks he might even become famous. He completes college with top honors. Three nationally known firms seek to employ him. He finally feels worthwhile. In the field of his choice he takes the job that pays the most money, has the best fringe benefits, and offers good advancement possibilities. He is all for John and nobody else.

He marries a very popular girl and buys a fashionable house in the suburbs. His income gives him a great sense of security and achievement. He joins the country club and plays golf with very important businessmen and politicians. He feels he has "arrived." He has everything — expensive cars, a fifty-foot yacht, good-looking clothes, etc.

A New Despair

Slowly, he comes to the realization that there are no more worlds to conquer. His wealth has purchased him everything but lasting friendships. He feels alone and alienated. He has been so busy getting to the top that he has failed to see his marriage crumbling. He never had time for his wife and children and he suddenly realizes there are a lot of pleasures he missed — the really important ones — having to do with family. He feels a vacuum. In the midst of all the success, honors, triumphs, and trophies, he feels an emptiness.

In the depth of his despair he remembers a Scripture he had long forgotten: "A man's life does not consist in the abundance of his possessions" (Luke 12:15). His soul once again begins to thirst after the nourishment that has no price. He questions the meaning and origin of life. He is plagued with the need for answers to the mysteries of life.

Free at Last!

He suddenly realizes that there must be something about his faith that he didn't grasp before. As he rediscovers the Word of God, the split or breach in his personality starts to heal. He begins to realize that God loves him as an individual and that he is really worth much in God's eyes. The rigid dos and don'ts, the legalism, and his superficial godliness begin to give way to a realistic relationship with Christ. He discovers that Christianity is a mystical union with Christ, an ongoing relationship that he doesn't have to earn.

He is no longer concerned with how many chapters a day he reads in the Bible, but rather in experiencing fellowship with God through Christ, feeling His presence, and receiving guidance for his daily life. One verse that burns in his soul may be enough spiritual food for a whole day or more. He also finds that praying is not just a formal ritual, but an unbroken communication. He comes to understand the meaning of 1 Thessalonians 5:17, "Pray continually." He talks to the Lord everywhere he goes — walking, driving, working, playing. Prayer is no longer a compulsive duty, but a spontaneous privilege.

He worships the Lord in the midst of his secular life, too, because he suddenly realizes that secular life is not necessarily sinful. He finds also that one man's spiritual writings appeal to him for a period of time, and then later he may find another man's writing meets his needs better. Sometimes he thirsts for doctrinal truth, other times for enrichment of his devotional life. The most important thing in his life is searching for that which will meet all the needs of his delicate, spiritual relationship with God and others. He finds truth, beauty, and goodness in other people, in nature, in the church, and in almost every aspect of his daily life. Christianity, at last, becomes for him a life of balances — the unifying ingredient that imparts meaning and purpose to his life.

John has come full circle. He has traveled the path from faith to doubt to faith — only, now his faith is a mature faith. He knows that Christianity is not "instant" happiness. He knows that the happiness and joy of the Christian life is provided by God, through Christ. God gives him the strength to surmount his difficulties; he never needs to feel alone or alienated. He is like many people today who have found the key to successful living.

Fulfillment in life is achieved through the development of abilities that can be used to help other people. Meaning and happiness come through the sense of being needed and used by God. This, in turn, comes through the completion of reasonable goals in combination with the divine will of God and a true appraisal of reality.

A Whole Person

John could find meaning only when he adjusted to situations as they really were. He had to abandon the exalted standards he had created for himself, for these had brought only emptiness and guilt because he could not consistently follow the rules.

He matured as a Christian when the burdens of the "don'ts" were replaced by a dynamic, ever-present relationship with Christ who gave him a new freedom. John's self-concept and personality were strengthened when this took place. This new adjustment made him a whole person.

The story of John can be multiplied many times. Most of us know people whom we admire because they seem to be in command of every situation and lead a balanced life.

I am thinking now of a man, who in my estimation, fits the description well. I have known him for years and have noticed that he is neither too emotional nor too intellectual but blends the two together very well. He is not driven compulsively to read his Bible, to buttonhole everyone in his effort to witness for Christ. He does not feel guilty if he misses church once in awhile. In fact, he may even stay home deliberately if he is overtired or feels the need for quiet and change. He is neither driven to be always sociable nor is he withdrawn.

He reads his Bible, witnesses in a natural manner, and supports his church. He is neither overcritical nor naive. He freely voices his opinions and is not slavishly worried about what people think of him. There is a spiritual dimension to his life. Others feel it in his deportment. He relates well to saved and unsaved alike in the business world. He is not afraid to work out a business deal and make substantial money.

He enjoys his hobbies and especially his home. He is kind to his wife and family and considers their opinions. He is not a dictator but is a solid, strong leader. There is a consistency about him in church and at home. He loves sports and is well versed in politics, the stock market and other world affairs. His life exemplifies the "abundant life" that Christ came to offer all of those who receive Him.

How refreshing it is to see a truly well-adjusted Christian. He is a credit to Christ and the church. This kind of a person exists only where the ego in his personality is strong and able to adjust. Such a person has a proper perspective of himself, reality in the external world, spiritual values, and God.

12

Marks of a Mature Christian

The Bible Provides the Best Pattern for Life

IN CHAPTER ELEVEN we saw that the well-adjusted person is characterized by a balanced life. The Word of God makes it clear that this is the pattern desired by God for the enhancement of our personal lives. The mature personality is best set forth in the Bible as possessing the "fruit of the Spirit" (Galatians 5:22, 23): "But the fruit of the Spirit is love, joy, peace, longsuffering, gentleness, goodness, faith, meekness, temperance: against which there is no law."

The Highest Good

We see from this Scripture that the first mark of a mature Christian is *love*. The idea of loving some people and hating others is not really consistent either with psychological or spiritual teaching. We may become angry at some person for what he does, but we should possess the virtue of loving the person, whether we approve of his acts or not.

Jesus points this out as a quality of a mature person when He suggests that we are to love God, ourselves, and others — including our enemies. The popular singer may become wealthy singing about love, but in real life he may not possess a loving nature. The young man driven by passion for his girl friend may think he is deeply in love when he is actually mistaking lust for love. But true love is the capacity to be just as concerned about the happiness, well-being, and feelings of the other person as we are about ourselves.

This is what Christ meant when He told husbands to love their wives as their own bodies. Love is a oneness; it is the ability to invest ourselves in another person and thus lose ourselves in another. The Scripture says, "For whoever wants to save his life will lose it, but whoever loses his life for me and for the gospel will save it" (Mark 8:35). Losing ourselves in the loved ones, living for their happiness, and doing what will please them helps us find ourselves. A stable relationship is built for the ego to communicate with and, in return, the person's love needs are met.

This is also true in the spiritual sense. Investing one's life in Christ, loving Him, worshiping Him, and serving Him gives man a relationship that will stabilize him through time and eternity. Human relationships are limited by time, whereas our relationship with Christ is for all time. What a comfort it is for a person to accept Christ, receive eternal life, and experience a living and abiding relationship on earth as well as hereafter. When we realize that all human relationships are transitory, we come to fully appreciate Jesus Christ who the Bible says is "the same yesterday and today and forever" (Hebrews 13:8).

Little Things Can Mean a Lot

The second mark of the "fruit of the Spirit" is *joy*. The mature person is capable of facing and handling conflict. He can accept the everyday problems of life and reach satisfactory conclusions without experiencing anxiety. He experiences life in its fullest sense. He feels, reacts, and adequately responds.

Life and nature in their simplest forms — such as the flower, the sunset, the butterfly, and the soft breeze — have meaning for him. He doesn't require expensive emotion-packed entertainment to get enjoyment out of life. He finds joy in a child's smile or a quiet moment of meditation. He can relate to people on an individual basis in spite of the crowded conditions and fast pace of our modern society.

I suppose it would be fair to say that a person who is in deep depression would be the exact opposite of a joyous person.

A Christian worker once came to me confiding that she had tried to take her own life on several occasions. "I tell my people that Christ is the secret of joy and yet I feel down all the time," she said. She was sullen, her speech was slow, and deep lines creased her face. Her life was miserable, yet she was supposed to be a Christian. As we talked about many of the deeply repressed and painful experiences in her life, her problems were worked through and her emotional stability was seen to improve rapidly and to mature. It was at this point that she had a new smile on her face and could carry the message of Christ to others.

Christians frequently are unable to experience or communicate joy. They may even know that rejoicing is a scriptural imperative, but for some reason, this emotional expression cannot be expressed. It is very likely because the individual has not matured emotionally and, as in the case of this woman, needs to find release for repressed feelings.

Be Right With the World

The third mark of the spiritually mature person is *peace*. You've heard the remark "Never have we talked more about peace and had so little of it." The mature man is not constantly seething with hostility. He has moved upward beyond this stage. He is at peace with himself and with his neighbors.

This does not mean he is a Caspar Milquetoast or a "doormat." He is capable of anger, speaks out against injustice, and tries to correct wrongdoing. He puts things in their proper perspective, however, and his anger is justified in proportion to the wrong deed or action. In his Christian life, he has made peace with God through Christ.

Extend Yourself

The fourth mark of the mature Christian is *longsuffering*. Longsuffering implies patience and endurance and is a great virtue for the ego. The small child hasn't the ability to wait for what he wants. When he decides he wants something, he wants it "right now." Usually, if he doesn't get his way, he throws a temper tantrum or starts whining. His ego is not able to organize and control the urges that arise within the body. A person who has a mature ego realizes that immediate satisfaction of a desire is not always as pleasurable as expected nor as long-lasting as waiting for the right thing at the right time.

For example, a man with a strong, mature ego might turn down an extra day off from work in order to combine it with his regular vacation. The mature person will hold his speech until an appropriate time. Even if he is deeply offended by a remark, he will consider the source, the timing, and the mood and will try to analyze whether it was meant as a personal affront or not. He will admit the hurt but control the retaliation.

Job's wife, for example, had poor control of her impulses when she said, "Curse God, and die" (Job 2:9). Job admitted the tremendous pain and testing, but held out until God vindicated and rewarded him.

A man came to one of my marathon sessions some time ago saying that his marriage was going down the drain. His wife was not a Christian. He said this was their problem. "If she would only realize that the man is the head of the house and the wife is to be subservient in all things — there would be no problem," he said. He was coming to the marathon only to help his wife, since he was a Christian. He had no problems, he thought.

He quoted Scripture profusely and as he talked, his own selfish, hostile disposition manifested itself. As others reacted to him, he was abrupt. He had no regard for their feelings. He did not demonstrate love in his manners, talk, or attitude in relationship to his wife, yet he talked constantly about how much he loved her.

True love is longsuffering and patient and considers the other person as he considers himself. A mature person is able to endure another's immaturity.

Source of Real Strength

The fifth mark of maturity is *gentleness*. Modern translations might use the word "kindness." This does not imply a weak and effeminate personality. Gentleness refers to a strong, yet warm and loving, personality.

I have had at least a normal amount of dental work in my life, by two different dentists. Both did good work. With one I could completely relax and with the other I always felt up-tight. The difference is that one was gentle and the other was not. The one who was not seemed insensitive to my pain when he was drilling. At times he even seemed rough and jerky.

The other dentist was completely different. He was gentle. It was as if he was working on himself and knew just how far to go. He would also ask "Does that hurt?" or "Tell me if I'm pressing too hard." He was a strong man but he was gentle.

Strength is too often equated with sternness or rigidity, but as we begin to know and understand people, we see that the truly strong man is also gentle. He does not use a show of strength to cover up for weakness. He is a flexible, understanding person who is easy to talk to and who is not harsh in his manner and attitudes.

Doing Things for Others

The sixth mark of maturity is *goodness*. In the Scriptures, gentleness and goodness sometimes seem to be the same thing. But goodness is to be equated more with human kindness in the sense of active benevolence or doing things for others. The emphasis is, therefore, on one's good deeds.

A person who feels good about himself will do good things for other people. An emotionally disturbed person who feels all tied up inside is battling his own emotions to such an extent that he cannot feel good toward people in his world. Instead, he will be cranky, demanding, bossy, selfish, and stingy. His acts will be the opposite of a well-adjusted, mature person who is anxious to do things for others.

True in All Endeavors

The seventh mark of the mature Christian personality is *faith*. Some translators render the word "faithfulness." Because of his trust in Christ a "faith-ful" person is consistent and fair in his business dealings and with his family. He is steady, dependable, and trustworthy. By contrast, the immature person, who cannot face the pressures or problems of making decisions, will change jobs, change localities, and change churches. He is never satisfied. His marriage will always be in jeopardy because, instead of facing reality, he runs from it. He is like the ostrich that buries its head in the sand and thinks it's well-hidden.

> Some time ago a man called me from his factory, wanting a character reference on a man who had applied for a job. He said, "You have no idea how hard it is to find good help today. A man may look good in the personnel office but when he comes to work, the newness wears off very soon. He may not show up one day, he may be consistently tardy, or he will 'goldbrick' on company time."
>
> I was sorry to have to report to this caller that the man seeking the job, in my opinion, was too immature and would not fit the qualifications of the type of man wanted for that position. Although he had the experience and the intelligence, he was not a faithful person. He could not be relied on. A person who has strong faith is consistent and can be relied on to be faithful in all his relationships in life.

The mature Christian will manifest different qualities. He will be a very responsible person. He will have very good relationships with people and his emotional roots with those he knows will be deep. He will not be a shallow, superficial person. His friendships will abide through the years. His relationship with God will be consistent. He does not worry and doubt, but believes and trusts. Because he has *faith* he is trustworthy and dependable.

In Harmony With Self and Others

The eighth mark of the mature Christian is *meekness*. This kind of person is moderate. He can endure hurt or injury without resentment. He is characterized by humility. He neither buries his talents nor overemphasizes them. He makes contributions in accordance with his true abilities. He fits in well with other people. He is willing to function within his capacity, and knows his limitations. He does not overextend himself by trying to please others at all times.

He may be likened to the mighty stallion who has crushing strength and mighty speed, yet has been tamed by his master. Even with its strength and capacity for speed, the horse may be quieted. Even a child can pat it on the head. Many emotionally immature people are very rebellious against any authority — that of law, the Bible, the church, the police, or government. They don't want rules. They don't want anybody telling them what to do.

The meek person can work with others as a team. He can fit into his slot and realizes that as a part of a team he can achieve great things. His strength is organized for the good of the whole. Only the mature person can truly live in this kind of harmony with others.

Strive for Balance

The last mark of the "fruit of the Spirit" is *temperance,* or self-control. The temperate person's ego is in complete charge of his actions. He is not enslaved or controlled by the urges of his physical drives. He can control his eating, his pleasure, his spending, his habits; yet he can accept himself and enjoy the finer things of life. He is not an extremist. He evaluates both sides of the question before he makes a value judgment. He is sensitive to himself, his needs, and others' needs. But he realizes that *temperance* does not mean a denial of pleasurable living.

> One day a Christian man from a rural area came to our Center saying, "I'm one bundle of ambivalence." He illustrates the person whose controls are lost. "I love and I hate the same people — especially the ones that I am close to. I feel torn up all the time on the inside. Is there any way to get rid of the hate so that I can just love and accept my fellowmen for what they are? I feel like a hypocrite who loves on the surface but is cursing everybody on the inside. I feel like what the Bible says, 'A house divided against itself cannot stand.' "
>
> When I examined a number of experiences with him in his earlier life, he gained insight and was able to mature into a fine, controlled Christian.

Another patient once came to me. She was the epitome of the uncontrolled person. She said,

> "I do everything without even thinking it through. I spend money impulsively. Whether I need a new dress or not doesn't seem to matter. If I am in the mood for a new dress, I just buy it. I also impulsively tell people off. I speak and then think later. Sometimes I make a real fool of myself. I know I should hold my weight down but I can't seem to leave the refrigerator door alone. When I order something that is to be delivered in the future, I just can't seem to wait. I want it now."
>
> This young lady eventually began therapy. After a period of time, she learned to think things through. Whereas her life had been dominated by emotion only, now she blended her decisions with intellectual controls. In the process of time she became a mature person with a balanced control over even her immediate wants.

This is the mark or goal of the controlled person. The personality is so integrated that self-control becomes a way or pattern of life.

Such a life is possible or this characteristic would not have been included as one of the evidences of a Spirit-led life. We remember well a trip we once took with a man who perfectly demonstrated this mark of maturity.

> I spent a week with him. You get to know a lot more about a man when you live with him for a week than when you only meet him socially when he is on his best behavior. Before we left on the trip he showed good judgment in planning it. He was able to laugh at his mistakes. When we were together, he could let his hair down and let his emotions flow freely. He knew his limitations. When he sensed that I wanted to go one way and he another, he was able to give part way as I had to give part way. We both enjoyed the trip, felt relaxed, and came home refreshed. He truly was a temperate person who knew himself and had self-control.

For Christians Only?

Many Christians are troubled by the fact that an unbeliever seems to demonstrate the characteristics of the Spirit-controlled life more than some believers who are always striving for it. Our experience shows this to be true.

The psalmist Asaph faced this same query about the ungodly when he said, "They have no pangs; their bodies are sound and sleek. They are not in trouble as other men are; they are not stricken like other men" (Psalm 73:4, 5). He was saying, "These people can even curse God and live corrupt lives, yet they aren't filled with nervous tensions and conflicts as I am." He even admitted that his faith was weakened. If Asaph were living today he might say, "I wonder if it pays to be a Christian. Is there any truth or reality in the Christian life, or is the Christian actually worse off because of his faith?"

To understand this paradox, we must remember that the Lord sends rain on the just and the unjust alike. If an unsaved person has warm, loving parents whom he can trust, this gives him a good basis for relating to people. Hence, he will be a very well-adjusted person emotionally. Also, if he is physically healthy, he will not need medical help as does one who is ill.

On the other hand, the Christian who has cold, rejecting parents will find it difficult to relate to people. Therefore, he may need therapy to help him become a well-adjusted person emotionally.

No matter who he is, a person must face his problems wherever he is. A Christian and a non-Christian can both have physical or emotional problems. The difference is that the Christian has the Lord to help him through his troubles, to give him wisdom, and to direct him to the people who can help him. Christ also gives him reasonable guidelines from the Scriptures, by which he may pattern his life.

Never Give Up

Neither emotional nor spiritual maturity is ever perfected in any of us. We have high moments and low moments, our "ups and downs," as it were. Certain traits keep recurring in most of us that remind us that we still have a long way to go to attain maturity. We must try to accept ourselves where we are, as Christ has accepted us where we are.

If we don't, we shall be plagued by a nagging sense of guilt that will destroy our peace of mind and threaten our ego. It is in Christ that we find the challenge to grow, for He has promised us that someday "we shall be like him, for we shall see him as he is" (1 John 3:2). This should encourage us to strive to continue our "growth in grace," knowing that someday all the emotional and spiritual problems will disappear. We will then be perfect and complete.

Psychology and the Work of the Holy Spirit

A truly, Spirit-led Christian will mature as he proceeds down the path of life. But this is no guarantee that he will not have problems.

> I'm thinking of a man who came to me very much in a state of anxiety because he thought he was going crazy. He stated that he was Spirit-filled. But he had the growing feeling that the more he yielded to the Spirit, the more he felt he was losing his mind. Although he felt guilty about coming to me, having been warned against it by his minister, he decided he couldn't go on the way he was. I am happy to say that this man worked out his problems, which were strictly psychological, and is serving God today in his local church.

Some people tend to use a spiritual experience as a defense against being emotionally involved with the world. The Holy Spirit should never be used as a crutch to escape from emotional involvement in the world. Some people seem to brag about their experience and appear to go off on some kind of "trip," much like the youths who seek thrills through drugs. A true, Spirit-filled Christian will talk about Christ and not so much about a mere subjective experience. The true work of the Holy Spirit involves much more than an emotional experience. He teaches, guides, and motivates people. And the Spirit points always to Christ. He does not lead us to go around talking about a "Holy Spirit experience." Our emphasis is on Christ. "He will bring glory to me" (John 16:14), says Christ concerning the work of the Holy Spirit.

It also must be said that a Spirit-controlled Christian will be empowered to strengthen healthy reality relationships with other human beings. If a spiritual experience of some kind or other takes us out of the world and takes us away from facing our problems, it is not the true work of God. A life truly led by the Holy Spirit will never lead a person away from reality.

Wherever the work of the Holy Spirit is in evidence in a person's life, there will be deep involvement with people. Philip was led by the Spirit into the wilderness to talk to a man (Acts 8). People often become depressed. One reason is that they dissociate themselves from people. Ultimately, the only effective and permanent answer to the problem of discouragement is the indwelling power of the Holy Spirit who will constantly help us relate to people.

Some Christians have developed the feeling that psychological techniques limit the power and influence of the Holy Spirit. But the Spirit is able to work through and utilize many of the techniques used to help people. At the same time it must be clear that ultimately it is the Holy Spirit, and not any psychological techniques, who works in people's lives to convict them of sin. Also, we must not forget that psychological counseling is a tool in the church and must never become its main work.

We have dealt at some length with the similar goals of secular psychology and of the Spirit-filled Christian life. At this point the reader may feel that there is no difference between the Christian and the unbeliever. This is not the case. First of all, what the secular man has found is the validity of God's laws and yet he denies the Creator Himself. Secondly, there is a vast difference between the Spirit-filled Christian and the mature man of the world. The Spirit-filled Christian is in love with Christ. The change in his life that produces the fruit of the Spirit has taken place by his identification with Christ who exemplifies the essence of these fruits. The secular man can rise no higher than his identification with another imperfect human being.

Let us reiterate in conclusion. Psychological and spiritual maturity have a common goal: the development of the personality so that it is flexible and strong. The psychologist seeks to improve the person's ego by removing the blocks that hamper his interpersonal relations with other people. Christianity also is concerned about removing the conditions that keep men from meaningful personal relations and, in addition, it is interested in restoring man's relationship with God in Christ.

Spiritual growth extends beyond this life but we must remember that the new life with Christ begins here and now. This relationship assures us of a stable love-object that endures beyond time and eternity. Jesus calls it *everlasting life*.

PART III

Harmonizing Psychology and the Bible
As We View Ourselves

13

Does Psychological Therapy Have a Right to Exist?

Therapy Provides a Better Understanding of Ourselves
As Well As a Total Christian World View

ONE OF THE most pertinent issues facing the Christian today is the question "Can the Bible and psychology be reconciled?" Are therapy and theology compatible or do they contradict each other? Many people are troubled by the enormous gains and inroads of professional psychology. They feel, perhaps, that because of this the church and the Gospel face great competition in meeting people's deepest needs. "The church," they say, "has all the answers for man's problems." Therefore, psychology and professional therapy are being frowned upon in some Christian circles. The purpose of Part III, and this chapter, is to disclose the harmony between sound psychological discovery and knowledge with the Bible.

In its beginning, psychology dealt more with understanding behavior in man and underemphasized the spiritual conflicts. Psychology is a relatively new science that has experienced growth pangs. Sigmund Freud certainly was not concerned with the inner, spiritual elements of man. On the other hand, Carl Jung was a religiously oriented psychiatrist who believed that religious faith was indispensable to emotional health, particularly in the second half of life. William James and Karl Menninger were also profoundly religious men who viewed the individual as essentially free, with the capability of finding and being himself and taking responsibility for his own existence.

Extremes exist on both sides. A badly biased psychologist might express the belief that religion is the source of neurosis, and a well-meaning but misinformed minister might conclude that psychology is the work of the devil.

Much confusion exists. Therefore, this chapter sets forth several areas that are often overlooked or ignored by people who intensely, and rightly so, want to defend at all costs the Word of God and the spiritual dimension in man.

We stand, too, in that noble effort. But we wish to face all issues in an honest and open manner. We believe we can do this without violating or denying in any way the truths contained in God's holy Word.

Are All Emotional Problems Spiritual Problems?

We heard a pastor in a well-known southern California church say that all problems are strictly spiritual — the assumption being, of course, that if a person gets right with God, he will no longer have emotional problems.

A nationally well known Bible lecturer has gone on record as saying that "all problems are strictly spiritual or they are physical."

If these men are correct, this means that for your problem you need only one of two things. You need a doctor or a minister. If the doctor can't find anything wrong with you — by use of X-rays and corpuscle count — then you need a minister, because your problem is only spiritual. Thus they have ruled out any need for the psychologist.

The pastor of a well-known Gospel-preaching church gave a series of messages on "The Deeper Life." The church of which he is pastor has had intense Bible teaching for twenty-five years. I was in the service one night when the minister gave a very dynamic message on being yielded to Christ and having complete victory. He said that anyone can have such victory.

The interesting thing in his invitation was the question "How many of you here tonight don't have this victory but you really want it?" There must have been 800 to 1,000 people in that service and virtually every hand was raised. Wouldn't you think that after all these years most of those people would have found "victory" by now?

Now, I want to propose the possibility that some other factor must enter the total picture, for most of those folks have been seeking victory for years. If going to the altar and raising the hand hasn't worked for them, then doesn't it make sense to believe that other factors are at work in their lives — factors that they do not suspect?

A woman who had been brought up in that very church came to me for help one day. After looking at a number of different areas in her life, we found together that she had some things she didn't understand about herself. We worked them through and she said to me, "Three months of therapy have done more for me than the last thirty years in church have done."

So the point here I think is very clear. Hers was not a spiritual problem but an emotional one.

That other factor for consideration that is extremely important for understanding the total picture is the right of a person to evaluate himself with the aid and support of a trained counselor. "It is one man needing another man," as someone has well put it. We admit there are quacks and counselors who employ techniques that are unworkable and unscriptural. But this does not mean that all counseling and counselors are to be discredited. Our focus is on psychotherapy in this chapter, rather than other fields, such as educational or social psychology, that also deal with changes in behavior. Psychotherapy is emphasized because it uses a specialized tool or method to change or to strengthen human behavior.

We now turn to the reason why psychotherapy has a right to exist and is justified even in the life of a believing, surrendered Christian.

Therapy Is a Biblical Concept

First, the Bible itself grants the existence and need for such a field. In 1 Thessalonians 5:23 Paul says, "May your whole spirit, soul and body be kept blameless at the coming of our Lord Jesus Christ." Our body is physical. Our spirit is the spiritual part of us. We also have a third part, rendered "soul" in this text. In the original Greek the word in this passage is *psyche* from which we get the word "psychology." Paul identifies man as a threefold, functioning being — spirit, soul, and body — and he wants all of these preserved blameless until the coming of the Lord Jesus. (Some scholars use the term "spirit" and "soul" interchangeably, as both referring to the immaterial part of man. But all would agree that man is an emotional and spiritual being.)

Those who say psychotherapy does not have a right to exist leave out a significant area that the Bible discusses. We might call it the mind, or the center of man's emotional life. The apostle Paul places great significance on this aspect of the individual.

We cannot deny the need for the cultivation of man's physical well-being as well as of his spiritual health. But the emotional side of man also needs to be observed, analyzed, classified, and understood, in order to help people to become whole human beings.

The Greek word for "healing" frequently used in the New Testament is *therapeia,* from which we get our word "therapy." So it comes right out of the Bible. Is not emotional healing just as valid as physical healing when you consider that in the United States today one out of two hospital beds is occupied by a person with an emotional affliction? Just because we cannot see mental disease as we can an abcess or a tumor does not mean it isn't there. The point is that we can observe it through behavior; so it is a valid area of concern and it needs to be treated.

The Bible Teaches a Gift of Healing

Secondly, the Bible, in 1 Corinthians 12, emphasizes the fact that God has endowed each of us with spiritual gifts necessary to help sustain and maintain the body of Christ. One of those gifts is the gift of healing. It is right to interpret this to mean that Christians are not only to believe in Christ but also to develop their natural God-given abilities to relieve human suffering of all kinds. That is why God calls psychotherapists for a healing ministry, just as He calls a surgeon or a minister. Each has his own specialized field of concern.

The more we relieve human suffering, the more we will see spiritual lives improved. If the psychologist can help a nervous man overcome his crowd phobia so that he can go back and hear the Word of God and grow in grace, how can you say that what has been done is purely secular? There's a blending of the secular and the spiritual in rendering such a service.

> Looking back on my own life, I would say that if I have any one strong gift, it is this gift of counseling. There are several reasons why I know this.
>
> When I was a farm boy in Nebraska, I used to date girls. I always tried to "figure them out," although at the time I didn't even know what the word "psychology" meant! I asked them questions like this: "I'll bet you would like this," or "I bet you don't like that." They often blushed and said, "How did you know that?"
>
> Even in my early twenties, teenagers came to me for counseling and advice. It just seemed to come naturally and I liked it.
>
> When I entered the pastorate, I found that I didn't especially care for administration or the endless business at all the deacons' and trustees' meetings. I preferred helping people with personal problems. Soon ministers in other churches began referring people to me because they heard that I was good in counseling.
>
> Thereby I came to realize this gift that God gave me. Frequently today I am asked, "How can you take the burden of people's problems forty to fifty hours a week?" I couldn't do it if it were not a gift or calling. I actually thrive on it. I sometimes stay late in the evening caring for people and when the next day comes, I am as enthusiastic as ever about my work. I consider this a gift of intuition and insight, as well. So the ability to heal mental disorders is a very valid gift. God has given this gift to countless people.

God does use the various gifts of people to help His children. A person once said to me, "I don't want to go and get man's advice. I want God's advice. In fact, my pastor gave a lesson on how we need only to listen to God and not man." My answer was "Who were you listening to? Isn't your pastor also a man? You're just as much a man and God can use your gifts, too."

Every Christian psychologist thanks God for every faithful and Bible-believing minister. The latter has a very vital service to render in the lives of people and the community. If an individual has a spiritual problem — such as his soul's eternal destiny, divine forgiveness, a better understanding of Bible passages, and emotional comfort — he should go to a minister. Such a seeking soul will gain from a pastor. But there is also something else to consider.

If a pastor studied nothing but theology while another man exclusively studied psychology for nine years, wouldn't it be common sense to conclude that, when it came to mental disorders, the man who had nine years of training in psychology might have something to add to the one who had no such training?

Did not Jesus even recognize the specialized gifts of people when, for example, He told the man cured of leprosy, "Go show yourself to the priest and offer the sacrifice that Moses commanded for your cleansing" (Mark 1:44). So we see that Jesus did not Himself always treat every individual completely. He listened to their cases first and then in some instances made referrals because He wanted to provide them with an opportunity to verbalize their feelings to test their faith, to strengthen their witness, and to get an emotional release through forgiveness.

We can learn from this. It is best to utilize people's special gifts. We have accepted this in the medical field. We are wiser if we get the expert in other specific areas as well — the best certified public accountant because he knows bookkeeping, the best tax man because he knows taxes, the best real estate man because he knows real estate, etc. The world is very complex today. We depend upon people with specialties. God uses people in many different ways and God uses people to cure other people. In this manner, psychotherapy serves a vital role in serving the needs of the whole person.

Means for a Two-Way Communication

A third reason why psychotherapy is such an important field is that it actually provides a two-way communication, whereas the pulpit or the Bible is generally a one-way communication. In other words, God speaks to me from the Bible and through the pastor. But how do we have a chance to sift and digest the material if we don't have a chance to talk it out? Therapy is basically that. It is a means of talking things out.

In one of my seminars we once had a parent-teenager rap. Somehow the subject of hair came up. A long-haired kid stood up and spoke out harshly against the church. When he had finished, a mother spoke up and objected to such feelings. She was not sure that we should even have such open expressions in church. After the session was over she came up to me and said, "I really learned something tonight." I replied, "What did you learn?" "I learned that I didn't realize how strongly I felt about this subject until I started talking it out."

We believe this illustrates a very important principle. One person may not realize how depressed he is, how introverted he is, or how he has turned his feelings in. Another may not realize how deeply his mind is just running on one obsessive thing. Still another may not realize how angry he is at his parents and he may not even realize the guilt feelings he develops because of it.

The point is that we may not even know who we really are or what we really feel about anything until there is a chance to talk it out. We may hear all the sermons in the world but actually, in a sense, that tends to reduce our sense of identity, because we get only the preacher's viewpoints. Sermons have their place but the question is "How do we really feel about things?"

I learned this painfully a number of years ago when I heard a very powerful and elegant sermon preached at Moody Memorial Church in Chicago. It was so simple and so thrilling. I just understood and believed everything that was said. I decided to plagiarize. I was going to southern Illinois the next weekend and decided to give that exact message in a church there. But the message fell flat. When I started speaking, I thought I would be identifying emotionally with the preacher in Chicago. But when I was out there alone and giving his content, I realized I didn't feel the same way I did the week before. It just wasn't "me" at all and the sermon was a dud.

The point is that we need to have a two-way communication. Then we know our true feelings better. That is why the Dead Sea remains a dead sea. Everything goes in, but there is no outlet.

I am not interested in getting rid of pastors. I am not interested in getting rid of the ministry. I am not interested in saying the church has no right to exist. All of us need to become involved in our church and strengthen it as much as possible. The church is ordained of God and is the bride of Christ, but I believe that within the church, as well as in other areas, we definitely need the chance to express feelings.

When a kid, for instance, is allowed to talk his feelings out about his belief in God or why he has to go to church or the restrictions imposed by his church, then he begins to sift things out for himself by talking them through. Then he truly knows what he believes and becomes a distinct person.

So therapy in face-to-face situations serves a vital function. Actual communication is a key. This is well-illustrated by the little boy who was terribly frightened by a nightmare. His mother came running to his bed and said, "Darling, what is the matter?" He said, "Oh, Mommy, the ghosts and the goblins are after me." Mother said, "Sonny, don't worry about it. Jesus is going to take care of you." The little boy grabbed his mother by the hand and, trembling, said, "That's fine, mother. Jesus maybe can take care of me, but I need someone I can see and touch."

A person may say, "I just pray to God; I just want the *Lord* to meet my needs." Well, any way you want to look at it, "God is spirit" (John 4:24). Nowhere does the Bible suggest that we do not need to relate to human beings whom we can see.

The Bible says, "Carry each other's burdens, in this way you will fulfill the law of Christ" (Gal. 6:2). There is no greater or more blessed experience than being alone with God in prayer, whether we are interceding on the behalf of others or supplicating for ourselves. This can be a most meaningful spiritual exercise.

On the other hand, if a man's marriage is falling apart and all he does is pray about it, then it becomes merely a means whereby he doesn't have to deal with the issues on a "gut" level. Prayer becomes nothing more than an escape mechanism. Nothing can lead us into abstract fantasy more than a reclusive life of praying! Surely, God never intended that praying or reading the Bible be used as a cop-out in relating to people. The psychologist can help a man like that become a mature person so that he can properly face stress. Then prayer will take on a new perspective and meaning.

We're not going to be any stronger spiritually than we are in interpersonal relationships with people. And this is very dramatic, for example, in the case of a depressive. He feels that he is no good, no one loves him, and no one wants to be around an awful person like himself. Many times those who are Christians will say, "When I pray, I feel like my prayers bounce off the ceiling." Here the need for interpersonal relations comes into sharp focus. The greater the ability to share feelings with people, the more one will find that God is real and deeply personal.

This idea is expressed beautifully in 1 John 4:20: "If anyone says, 'I love God,' yet hates his brother, he is a liar. For anyone who does not love his brother, whom he has seen, cannot love God, whom he has not seen." Our love for God is measured in a real sense by our relatedness to fellow human beings. If we can't relate to people whom we have seen, then relating to God will be most difficult.

For those who say that all we need is the Bible, this verse provides a deep insight that is often overlooked by well-meaning Christians.

In intercommunication the psychotherapist is actually implementing the Bible. By listening to a person we practice the Bible, love our neighbor, and relate to him. Certainly Jesus' life was an example of personal involvement. Study the parables and narratives in the gospels; for example, the man by the pool at Siloam with his problem of thirty-eight years or the woman at the well of Sychar. Jesus is an example to us in psychotherapy and we should walk where He walked.

> A woman once told me, "I can't believe it! You have no idea the doctors I've been to with my terrible migraine headaches. But since I've been coming here to you in the last couple months, they have just totally disappeared. I've gone from healing meeting to healing meeting and from preacher to preacher, but you're the only one who really helped because you listened to me and I've talked these things out."

The Bible Is Not a Psychology Textbook

A legitimate issue to raise at this point is this: Doesn't the Bible have all the answers to every problem in a person's life? Many Christians believe that it does and thus the psychologist is considered to be evil or at least an unnecessary crutch.

But we must remember that the Bible is not a manual for emotional sickness. It is the textbook for sin-sickness. In the Bible we basically have the history of Israel and the birth and the life of Jesus Christ, the Messiah and Savior. From the book of Acts on, we have the Church as an outgrowth of the work of Christ's death, burial, and resurrection. Then in the book of Revelation the Bible ends with the final consummation of all things. It deals with the sin question and how to enter into God's "forever family." So the Bible is primarily interested in solving spiritual problems.

Emotional sickness deals with the distortions, the hurts, the frustrations that relate to man-to-man relationships. Bad relationships with people are cured only by right relationships with people. The woman who comes to us and says, "I can't accept Christ as my Savior; every time I begin to say the Lord's Prayer, 'Our Father in Heaven,' I freeze," may have more than just a sin problem. God has done her no harm. The problem may be that her father was a real beast. This illustrates that many times our human relationships affect our divine relationships.

We might compare the spiritual and the psychological to two train tracks. There is an illustration Dr. Donald G. Barnhouse gave when he lectured at First Presbyterian Church in Denver, Colorado, many years ago. He said that people keep wanting to know, "Is it predestination or 'whosoever will may come'?" He replied that he felt it is really not one or the other. It is like two train tracks; the only way to keep the train on the track is to have a rail set on each side. If you remove the left rail, you're going to fall into the left ditch. If you remove the right rail you're going to fall into the right ditch. So it is in the relationship between the spiritual and the psychological. The two do not contradict each other but go side by side, and you can follow the rails all the way to Chicago. It may appear to the reader that a cleavage still exists between the two tracks because they never merge. This is true, but they do not have to come together, for both are needed to give support to the train in order for it to fulfill its function. The tracks are parallel but yet there remains an integrated harmony between them.

We do need the Bible as a spiritual guide concerning what is right and wrong and the way to find salvation and forgiveness of sin. But we also need help from other sources as a guide and support for emotional health. This is not to say that emotional support does not exist in the Word of God. There is much emotion and feeling in the devotional content of the Psalms, for example, where Hebrew verbs often display extremely intense feeling, both in seeking help from God and in thanksgiving for what God has done in one's life. One specific example from Isaiah is found where the prophet, speaking of the great need for the development of a deeper relationship with God, relates emotional support to spiritual enrichment: "Thou dost keep him in perfect peace, whose mind is stayed on thee" (Isaiah 26:3). But if we accept only the Bible, we can drift off into fantasy and can get out of touch with people. If we emphasize only the emotional while excluding the Bible and share nothing but our feelings we can run into trouble, too, because we may be setting up our own criteria for reality rather than God's truth. So, if we ride the two tracks together, we will have a beautiful ride.

Furthermore, it is good to understand that the Bible was not communicated through emotionally disturbed people. Its truth was given to *rational* and *normal persons*. Was Isaiah on the verge of a nervous breakdown when God called him? No, there is not one person in all the Bible whom God called to do a job who was not emotionally equipped to carry it out. Suppose Abraham had had agoraphobia — a fear of open places — that might cause him to go into an anxiety attack? Do you suppose he would have been able to heed God's call and leave Ur of the Chaldees to go into the land of Canaan? Jonah did at first run the other way when he was sent to Nineveh, but he was without question capable of speaking in public. Now if every time Jonah spoke, his mind went blank because he had a fear of crowds, it's very doubtful that God would have called him to go to Nineveh. When he did get there, he cried out, walking up and down the streets of that enormous city and its surroundings, twenty-four miles in length, calling everyone to repent. He was such an effective preacher that even the king sat in sackcloth and ashes. Let's take Peter as another example. He had to be capable of love or Jesus would never had said to him, "Simon, son of John, do you love me?" (John 21:17). Christ would not have asked him this question if Peter had not had the capacity for giving or receiving love.

You can see from these examples the attention that God pays to the psychological as well as the spiritual capacities of men. Even during his more hysterical moments, Peter was a very sensitive and loving person who conscientiously wanted to do the right thing. We see this when Jesus said, "I want to wash your feet," and Peter said, "Oh no, I'm not worthy for you to wash my feet." Jesus replied, "Well, if I can't wash your feet, you're not a part of me." Peter responded, "Then pour it from top to bottom." You can see his tremendous emotional reaction to Jesus.

Also the Bible, then, as God's vehicle of truth, is given only to those who are able to receive it. Only those who are able to comprehend and respond to its claims of love are required to meet God's terms of commitment. A person who is deeply disturbed emotionally cannot do that.

So, then, to aid people with emotional problems we need to look to other sources, as well as to the Word of God.

All Truth Is From God

This leads us quite naturally into the next reason for the right of psychotherapy to exist. Truth is truth, no matter where we may find it. Therapy and counseling deal with the laws of human behavior that are discoverable and observable. Now the Bible, because it deals primarily with sin sickness, does not go into all of these other types of laws. But that does not make psychotherapy any less valid.

We may draw the analogy of the surgeon. The Bible does not provide him with the procedures for open-heart surgery, but that certainly does not invalidate the truth found in the field of surgery. Heart surgery is, therefore, not of the devil. In the same way, psychotherapy provides many answers to human needs and problems not set forth in Scripture.

This can be illustrated in many ways. The laws that get the astronauts to the moon are not necessarily discovered by Christians, nor are they found in the Bible. We do not see anything that contradicts the Scriptures in the laws of gravitation or aerodynamics that have permitted man to go to the moon. Is there anything in the Bible that says man will never be able to go 2,000 feet above the surface of the earth? Or does it say that man will never be able to travel beyond the speed of 700 miles an hour? Does it say that man will never travel to another planet? No, these laws are not mentioned in the Bible. The point is that man has discovered natural laws. We don't find Newton's law in the Bible, but we have found applications of it when we observe nature as it is.

In like manner, there are valid laws of human behavior that we do not get from the Bible. The natural laws that have been discovered tend only to confirm the Bible. God does not have to reveal them directly, for He has given man intelligence to find, state, and apply them.

So truth in any field will not contradict truth in other lines of thought, because all truth finds its origin with God. Truth is without qualification. God has never been against human research and has permitted man to make many wonderful discoveries, such as the Salk vaccine. But many of these truths are outside the scope of the truths in the Bible.

"Freud Is Not All Wrong"

It is good to keep in mind, too, that many of the natural laws of God have been discovered by non-Christians. This does not invalidate at all the essence of truth contained in their proven propositions. This means, for example, that if a godless man like Sigmund Freud has something to offer that is true, we must regard it seriously.

For instance, it was Freud who opened up to the world the concept of the unconscious mind and how it affects behavior. It was Freud who studied dream work, and especially chapter seven of his book *The Interpretation of Dreams* has been considered a classic by noted students of dreams today. Beyond a doubt, his insights have been widely used to alleviate human suffering in today's world. It was Freud whose technique of psychoanalysis was indispensable in helping us to understand and treat many forms of neurosis, especially the obsessional neurosis. And it was Freud who made a real breakthrough in terms of the psychic development of human beings. Probably the most controversial part of his theories revolved around sex and what he said about religion.

Before entering graduate school, I was warned about Freud's view on sex and that his goal was to take away man's conscience in relation to sin. This would mean, for instance, that if a man went through Freudian analysis he'd come out with loose moral standards and would be encouraged to act out sexually. After I got in school, much to my amazement, I discovered that he was not pushing free-love at all and that his teachings about sexuality revolved around what he called the "psycho-sexual development" of a person or the pleasure zones of the body, for instance, the mouth. I think it is unfortunate that his view of psycho-sexual development has been confused with popular godless theories of sexual lust rather than with psychological or physical development. So I discovered that it is much easier to criticize Freud than to understand him. My schooling also helped me to develop an appreciation for his insights.

Our experience with Christian people who seek psychoanalysis is that at the end of analysis they are back in church with a new mature perspective and they have a more satisfying and fulfilled Christian life. Their analysis has actually strengthened their faith. And more often than not, those Christians in analysis who no longer attend church and even develop an agnostic philosophy of life are influenced by a godless analyst who has projected his godless attitudes into their minds rather than helping to resolve their neurotic problem. In such cases the fault does not lie with the analysis but with the analyst.

Again, sometimes people who purport to be Christians jump quickly into analysis and it may be discovered that they had no faith at all but were using Christianity or religion as an escape only for neurotic reasons.

"Freud Is Not All Right"

Freud's main problem, as is true of most secular men, was that he tended to speak as an authority in a field he knew nothing about. He believed that all religion is no more than an unresolved infantile dependency-need for parents. This is preposterous. It is true that often people do use religion as an escape from the harsh realities of this world, but we know that millions today and throughout history have had a fulfilling and meaningful relationship with God in their lives to help them cope with life. Presidents, governors, senators, corporation heads, and other emotionally mature people have looked to God in faith for normal strength and help in the time of need.

But our disagreement at certain points with a man's view does not necessarily invalidate or discredit the good he has done. We need to incorporate his contribution into the larger body of truth. Rather than engaging in a tirade against all non-Christian systems of mental healing, Christians need to be critically appreciative of the thoughts of secular people, for God may have given them certain insights that are of great benefit to man. We must be broad enough to learn from all disciplines, whether the authors are believers or not. We need the unbeliever's help, too, in the enormous task of trying to better understand human behavior as well as to find the best approaches in rendering aid to the emotionally distressed. Let us learn to use what is real, practical, and workable for the glory of God, no matter who says it! We must integrate it into a workable system of therapy that leaves our faith in the center of our achievements.

The laws of human behavior, as expressed in the field of psychology, are nothing more than one facet of God revealed to man. If we find a secular theory of psychotherapy that genuinely heals people, there can be nothing in that principle that will in any sense contradict the

Bible. If through secular knowledge, for example, we can build a conscience or help a person who is rigidly bound by too severe a conscience and sense of guilt, then as Christians we must have an open mind and honestly regard such truth as having its source in God. Psychology, then, cannot be as evil as some Christians have tried to make it out to be.

For Every Illness There Is a Corresponding Treatment

Another major reason for the right of psychotherapy to exist is that it meets a specific need that no other level of knowledge can provide. Every illness has its corresponding treatment or antidote. For example, the American Indians found that a certain plant that was always growing near poison ivy served as an adequate medication when they rubbed it on the area affected by contact with the poison ivy plant.

In spiritual matters, if one feels aimless in life, there is a corresponding treatment: salvation through the blood of Christ. If he receives Christ, he stands before God as though he had never sinned. Now there is only one treatment for the disease of sin. But this can't apply to every illness, just as not every illness can be treated with digitalis. If a doctor would attempt to use digitalis for every illness, he wouldn't practice medicine very long. So, if a Christian, following God's Word, feels that his anxiety is about to "drive him up a tree" because he can't get relief by spiritual means, then he needs psychotherapy, not spiritual therapy.

We may put this another way. Every sphere of truth has its own "universe of discourse" or set of data in which it is valid. Mathematics is valid only in the "universe" of mathematics. Science is valid only where the scientific method may be applied. Each discipline has its own criteria for arriving at truth. This is why the college sophomore in his search for God never finds Him in a mathematical equation, test tube, or at the logical conclusion of a syllogism. He's looking in the wrong "universe of discourse." God is discovered only in the larger unseen "universe," for He is spirit (John 4:24).

There are certain factors about human behavior and motivation that form their own universe of discourse. This is the field of professional psychotherapy. This is precisely why it is sometimes useless to tell a neurotic or psychotic person to follow all the advice given from the pulpit. We're reminded of a little record that our kids used to play, a cute rendition with a reminder to "read your Bible, pray every day" etc. It was almost an echo of what we hear sometimes from our pulpits as the panacea for everything. Did it ever occur to you that if a man has deep pathological anxiety, he can't even concentrate long enough to read the Bible? He is so distraught with internal conflicts that his attention span is too short.

A man came to my office having heard a famous lecturer say that if a person memorized sections of Scripture, perverted sexual feelings would disappear. But it hadn't worked for him. He simply had no control over these impulses that were driving his life. Good as memorization of Scripture is, it is only a simplistic answer. The man needed more than this to control his pathological patterns. We've learned that such a person needs to develop an ego identity with a strong personal touch with another human being. Another "universe" is needed to fulfill the total need.

Then, many times a person comes to us whose parents tried to solve all the problems of life by only reading the Bible and praying. Many of these patients find that their hatred for such spiritual things is so great that they had to talk it out before they could get back to a spiritual plane where they were able to read the Bible and pray effectively. That's where therapy comes in.

For instance, consider the question of smoking. There are patients who are so orally inclined or have such a need for oral intake due to a deficiency of love in early childhood that if you took the cigarettes away from them too rapidly, they might go into a psychosis. Maybe it would be a sin for you to smoke because you don't need tobacco. But for this kind of person, who has a neurotic need that goes much deeper than mere habit, it would be bad advice to remove this crutch even though you may think it to be a bad crutch. If, from a spiritual point of view, he is made to feel like it is a sin to smoke, then he is made to feel as though he is losing God, as well as potentially triggering a psychotic episode.

Therapy has its rightful place because for many people it fills a need that cannot be fulfilled or met in any other way. For many it is the only treatment that works for certain ills. It helps a person grow naturally at a rate that is just right for him.

Psychotherapy Provides Means for Finding the Source of Illness

Again, psychotherapy has a distinct right to exist because its methods help to analyze the past life of an individual where aberrations, hang-ups, and neurotic patterns develop. Many people say that the thing they object to about psychotherapy is that it is not necessary to delve into one's past. They say, "The past is under the blood; let's just forget about the past and go on from here." But how can this be? If there are hangovers from the past that are creating the conflicts in the present, you cannot thoroughly solve the present problem by ignoring the past.

The Bible tells us in Proverbs 22:6 that we should train up a child in the way that he should go and when he is old he will not depart from it. That is just fine for the child who is well-adjusted because of good training and upbringing. But suppose we have a child who had the wrong kind of training that is causing him all kinds of trouble *today*. Or suppose he received virtually no training at all. Do we then not need to lift things out of the past and examine what was there that went wrong, trying to build a bridge and give him a sense of right identity that he never did get as a child? If no one showed this child the way or gave him proper love, which should have been a part of training, then there are going to be scars. He does need to know the way and we have to remove the bad emotional reactions in the past that may be blocking adjustment in the present.

A woman once said to me in therapy, "I feel like a little girl. I feel very sheepish about this but I came to group therapy without an appointment. I just wanted to see you. When you weren't here, I felt terribly embarrassed. After all, I'm a grown woman — but I feel like a little child. Sometimes I feel like an adolescent girl who just wants to go out with fellows and hold hands. Here I am, married and a mother with four children at home. How stupid this all is."

Psychotherapy is a second chance for people like this to relive childhood or the adolescent period to work out bad reactions, traumas, etc. Only, this time it is much safer because of the conducive environment. So, it provides a wonderful chance to relearn feelings in better perspective.

The minute we say this, there are always those who reply, "But doesn't the Bible say in Philippians 3:13, 14 that, like Paul, we should forget those things that are behind and reach for those things that are ahead? Let's forget those things and let's just go on from now to the future." To be biblically accurate, we have to take every passage in context. Notice what Paul said relative to forgetting the things in the past and reaching for those things ahead. What was he talking about? He was talking about all of his earthly credentials that he had been trusting to get him to heaven. He had trusted in the merit of his good works and he acknowledged the tendency to do so as a Christian. In the same chapter, verses 4-9, he renounced the validity of good works as a basis of salvation, both before he became a Christian and after. He said, "If anyone else thinks he has reasons to put confidence in the flesh, I have more; circumcised on the eighth day, of the people of Israel, of the tribe of Benjamin, a Hebrew of Hebrews; in regard to the law, a Pharisee; as for zeal, persecuting the church; as for legalistic righteousness, faultless. But whatever was to my profit I now consider loss for the sake of Christ. What is more, I consider everything a loss compared to the surpassing greatness of knowing Christ Jesus my Lord, for whose sake I have lost all things. I consider them rubbish, that I may gain Christ and be found in him, **not** having a righteousness of my own that comes from the law, but that which is through faith in Christ — the righteousness that comes from God and is by faith."

These verses deal with the issues of salvation and service for Christ. There is no correlation here with the thought or the idea of forgetting past emotional traumas or problems of that particular nature.

But then someone else says, "I know some people who keep thinking and talking only about the past. All they do is look at themselves, feeling sorry about the past. If they would just forget themselves and move on, they wouldn't have the problem." Well, let us point out that morbid thoughts like those are an evidence of illness. In fact, that is one of the things that drives people to therapy.

One of psychotherapy's functions is to help people gain insight into the traumas of the past, enabling them to relate them to present behavior so that they will be able to change in the future. Many people misunderstand this. They think therapy drives them back to live in the past. This is not true. The role of therapy is to help people become aware of the fact that the past is still with us while we are living in the present. So the past needs to be dealt with in the present. That is utilizing the past and making it serve us in the future. So the past is important.

If God had no interest in the past, why is it recorded in the Bible that Rehoboam was unwise when he forsook the wisdom of the old men and took the wisdom of the young men? What He intimated was that the old men had a lot of past experiences behind them and their wisdom was valuable. If we are to forget the past, why did God give us so much space in the Bible concerning the history of men and nations? In fact, it says in Romans 15:4 that we have all these things written in the Old Testament as examples so that we don't walk into the same pitfalls. If we are to forget the past, why did Jesus tell His disciples at the Last Supper, that as often as they eat the bread and drink the wine of the sacrament, they were to do so in *remembrance* of Him? (1 Corinthians 11:23-26).

Now, if a person uses the past only as a defense against present problems, he has a morbid, sick introspection. He is nothing but a person with a neurotic need. He tries to get attention from other people, wanting people to feel sorry for him. In psychotherapy it sometimes is a very frightening thing to look at the past because there are many hurts and terrible traumas that have to be worked through. Sometimes it takes a strong person to face the past, but in facing the past and dealing with the "paper tigers" there, he will find God to be very real and a great support in the present. Then he no longer has to live emotionally in the past to satisfy his present needs.

Closely related to this subject about the past is the question of the unconscious. Some psychologists even talk about the "science of the unconscious."

When I was in the pastorate, many people came to me with guilt problems. I showed them all the verses in the Bible about confessing guilt and finding forgiveness. But sometimes I noticed some people never really knew what they were guilty about. "I feel like I've committed a crime." "I feel that I've done some awful act and I really don't know what it is." I used to say, "All right, the Bible says that the blood of Christ covers all sins and we should pray about it." We'd pray and confess and seek forgiveness. It was marvelous! But when they got home, frequently the guilt was there again.

We have now learned from clinical experience that until one brings out of the unconscious what is there so that the person becomes aware of it and is able to link it up with the present, he is never going to be able to get the spiritual resolution or forgiveness he needs. You just can't feel forgiven for something unless you know what it is that has made you feel guilty.

So then, we frequently have to delve into the past, and psychotherapy serves as a wonderful and unique tool with which to accomplish this.

The New Psychotherapies

For many years about the only professional approach to therapy was Freud's psychoanalysis. Today there are many modifications of his view as well as entirely new approaches to counseling. An enormous revolution that is going on these days is intended to make psychological help more effective and available to broader groups of our population. One well-known modern counselor has more or less rejected the old school with these words: "Freud said people do things because they are sick. Today we are finding that people are sick because they keep on doing the same things. The former offers little hope. Today we hope to change the present mode of behavior in people, and their illness will leave them." The question may be raised whether these new methods represent progress or are merely fads. But there appears to be mounting evidence that more and more people are finding help through them and we should keep an open mind toward them.

This search to discover new helping techniques seems to have begun during the 1920s with Karen Horney, who departed from the conventional psychoanalyst position. She said that present environment is as big a factor as the early years in a person's maturation. Many others — such as Harry Stack Sullivan, Alfred Adler, Carl Jung, and Erich Fromm — followed, believing that the classical approach was too time consuming and yielded too few successes.

Prominent among the new schools is the rational-emotive school of psychotherapy pioneered by Dr. Albert Ellis. He believes that emotion and thought are correlatives, or opposite sides of the same coin. Thought is always operative in connection with distressing emotion. Because we all carry our own inner styles of self-hurting, thought must be brought into strong play to change the forces that determined our past reactions to how parents were relating in our formative years. This view has wide acceptance.

Perhaps the major entry in our day is Behavior Modification, with several offshoots. It may also be called the "Human Potential Movement." Such names as Abraham Maslow, Carl Rogers, William Glasser, Herbert Otto, Henry Link, and Erich Fromm have almost become household words. Maslow saw that within man there are great resources to help him become a self-actualized person or one who is aware of his present state and environment. Thus, man is not at the mercy of his past alone. More than twenty-five years ago Carl Rogers innovated a basic tool for reflecting feeling back to a person so that he could hear himself. Such reflections were to be packaged in a spirit of "total acceptance." William Glasser's Reality Therapy strongly emphasizes current behavior rather than events and feelings of the past. In therapy he sought to get his clients to make commitments or contracts to do certain things which were part of a reasonable plan of action. Through his method patients are helped to become aware of what they are *doing,* rather than how they *feel* about it.

Thus, for a person in trouble or afraid, Behavior Modification analyzes the components of his fears and slowly but surely offers a sequence of vaccinations or desensitizations to the sufferer. It is not, therefore, important what causes his hang-up. It is important that he talk of his scare or of his anger toward his spouse, for example. Working from the base of experimental or behaviorial psychology, the proponents of this view utilize principles of reinforcement through reward and selective punishment of deprivation (if you are ten minutes late to the dining room, you lose two coins). For some, the supportive emphasis is of great help and this method of therapy has a wide following today.

The growth-center movement of the group or encounter therapies has grown by leaps and bounds across the United States. It uses a number of Gestalt techniques of developing warmth and enthusiasm through human contact, sensitivity, and caring in the hopes of facilitating growth. For some people who are not deeply disturbed this method has brought success.

Hypnotherapy introduced by Anton Mesmer is another comparatively new and popular means of therapy. Hypnosis does not constitute a closed system of therapy by itself, but rather an exceedingly potent and varied process that can be accommodated meaningfully and productively to a variety of therapeutic procedures.

Psychodrama or "collective counseling" presents a strong case among its many adherents. It appears to have its best results among alcoholics, stammerers, some neurotics, and people with sexual difficulties. Antonio Moreno in Vienna, Austria, appears to be the pioneer of this method of counseling.

Transactional Analysis is another very popular mode of therapy. It was first introduced by Dr. Eric Berne, a psychiatrist, in his book, *Games People Play*. "TA," as it is known in the profession, discloses that in each of us there are three ego states: those of parent, adult, and child. The theory sets forth the view that the parent in us is the do's, oughts, don'ts, shoulds, rules, regulations, etc. The adult is that part of us that acts like a computer. It takes in data, interprets it, and then comes out with an objective solution. The child is that part of us that is fun-loving, irresponsible, inadequate, manipulative, etc.

According to Berne, in our relationships with people we behave, respond, or act from one or another of these three states. The purpose of therapy in this method is to analyze these transactions to discover what part of us is reacting. TA attempts to strengthen the adult component by getting the individual off the hook of the past, making possible more real freedom and emotional maturity. This methodology presents a good cognitive approach for people who may be hard to draw out or who lack insight. It makes people work by looking inside themselves. It also provides another strength by offering a different vocabulary for the man in the street. It tones down some of the heavier psychological jargon by providing terms that are more familiar to people. Thomas A. Harris's best-selling manual of psychology, *I'm OK — You're OK*, has popularized this view and gained a large following.

The aforementioned theory and many other theories of approach for psychological help and growth have done at least one thing — they have broadened the horizons of knowledge and of the technology of helping. They have dispelled much of the stigma of emotional illness and have brought a new sense of caring for people who are hurting.

Therapy Helps Lead People to Christ

Finally, psychotherapy's existence is vital as a means for witnessing to Christ's redemptive love and plan of salvation, as well as ministering to man's other great needs in this life. Christ said that when we reach into the lives of others, we are an extension of His love and service. "I tell you the truth, whatever you did for one of the least of these brothers of mine, you did for me" (Matthew 25:40).

Through the medium of psychotherapy, the Christian counselor has a unique opportunity to introduce people to Jesus Christ. Unless we get to know people on a deep level and aid in healing their diseases, they're never going to want to come to Christ. Therapeutic counseling opens the door for needy souls to measure and respond to special care and concern, and this enhances the need for Christ.

Even if an individual doesn't wish to become a Christian, we have a genuine ministry to lessen his pain and his problems. We fulfill the law of Christ when we provide therapy that helps a man with his marriage and his children. If he has no interest in spiritual things, therapy can become an effective way to reach him for Christ. Even if he never comes to Christ, is this not a Christian ministry and service?

In conclusion, psychotherapy fills a great need today. It has a rightful place in the Christian community. And an appreciation of professional counseling as an arm of the local church can increase the Christian's total understanding of his world and his role in administering God's love for individuals who desperately need to experience life at its very best.

We believe that the field of psychotherapy and the spiritual domain are closely related and compatible because their goals are not dissimilar — they both seek to bring good and fulfillment, maturity and enrichment, and the ability to receive and give love in a permanent way so that life may bring the highest satisfaction and enjoyment possible.

14

Demon Possession or Mental Illness, Which?

Many Fanciful Ideas About Demons Abound. The Responsible Person Will Examine All the Evidence

FREQUENTLY INDIVIDUALS ARE referred to us because they are considered to be demon-possessed.

One of the tragic things that I met in my ministry to people is the emotionally disturbed person who is tagged by his church to be demon-possessed because of some odd and unorthodox behavior. Such was the case of Melissa. She was told by certain church members that they were praying that God would deliver her from the demons that were possessing her. Special prayer gatherings were held. She was brought before the elders of the church for their prayers. Finally, she was told by her pastor that there must be some point of surrender in her self-life that was needed before God would deliver her. She was also warned that psychologists were of the devil and that if she would go to a psychologist for help, this would be the last step in her surrender to Satan.

For months she went along with this thinking, but nothing ever happened to help her. One day she heard about our Center and that we were all Christians. In desperation she gave me a call. By this time she was being shunned by all her church friends, much like a person in Old Testament times when he was declared unclean.

After a short period of hospitalization with sustained medication, Melissa was able to talk about her problems, which were of a very early origin. She began to feel herself again, coming to realize that she was a person and that she really did exist. Her hallucinations disappeared and her relationships improved, especially with her family. Unbelievably, the biggest problem that we faced was getting her well-meaning church friends to accept her as a person and not to frighten or threaten her about the demon issue.

With a renewed emphasis today on the study of the spirit world, the question of demon possession looms very large in people's minds. Christians, too, want reasonable answers. The questions they are

127

raising really boil down to a two-part question: "Can the instances
of demon possession cited in the Bible be simply explained as mental
disorders? Aren't some forms of what the psychologist calls 'mental
illness' really demon possession?" These are valid issues and a thought-
ful and sincere person will want to obtain as many facts as possible
to find the answers.

Demons Have Always Intrigued Men

Throughout all the centuries of man's existence, he has always had
a keen interest in the unknown or spirit world. He has long associated,
for example, natural or personal catastrophes with the action of evil
spirits. When an individual demonstrated strange or abnormal behavior, exorcism or witchcraft were employed to get rid of the demons.
Occasionally, someone would advocate medicine as a treatment for
deviant behavior. But the heathen world, by and large, accepted, and
still accepts, the view that abnormal behavior is caused by the control
of some demonic spell or power. The abnormal person is a helpless
victim, held in the demon's grip.

The Christian Church also became vitally interested in the subject
— especially during the Patristic period and the Middle Ages, up to
the time of the Renaissance and the Enlightenment. You have heard
about the witch-burnings in both Europe and America. They were
the result of certain beliefs. The supposed witches were possessed by
evil spirits and therefore had to be exterminated, lest their influence
be felt by other people.

Although witchcraft existed in the Old Testament period (Exodus
22:18, "You shall not permit a sorceress to live"), it was revived in
opposition to Christianity and the early churches. Many of the witch
cults worshiped Satan and demons, as well as their own fertility gods.
They performed bizarre pagan rites and rituals in complete opposition
to the accepted concept of God and Christianity. Throughout church
history many people have been executed as witches. Many were
suspected because of their interest in scientific experimentation and
others because they were seeking God in meetings outside the established religious system. The witch hunts and cults reached their peak
in the sixteenth and seventeenth centuries.

Today many psychologists and many highly educated people in the
behavioral science field reject the possibility of demon influence or
possession. They would regard such beliefs as belonging to the most
primitive, ignorant, or superstitious people.

Demon Influence Today

We are finding in our world a tremendous resurgence of interest in
the power of evil. There can be no doubt about the fact that there is
an unusual amount of demonic influence. This may be the direct

fulfillment of a prophecy uttered by the apostle Paul in 1 Timothy 4:1, "But the Spirit clearly says that in later times some will abandon the faith and follow deceiving spirits and things taught by demons." This verse speaks about the hypocrisy of demonically inspired leaders. This does not allude directly to demon possession but it certainly emphasizes the heightened activity of evil spiritual forces arrayed against men toward the end of the present church age.

Again, in Revelation 12, we have the picture of the end time of human history as we presently experience and know it. This period will be characterized by an awesome increase in evil by Satan against Christ and His anointed ones.

Today we may be witnessing just the beginnings of such an unleashing of demonic forces on the earth. Satan-worship is experiencing a phenomenal growth. This is truly an indication of a step-up in demonic activity. It is alleged that devotees regularly celebrate the Black Mass and have orgies. They usually believe that the attainment of perfection and the experience of the divine come through an ecstasy achieved in a sensual orgy, which is likely to involve sexual practices, nudity, homosexuality, and the use of drugs.

Over the altar in their houses of worship hangs a cross upside down and a picture of the devil, half-human, half-beast. The high priest wears an inverted cross. They have an actual liturgy. They shout, "Shemhamforash," which is probably the most powerful word uttered in Satan-worship. According to the Talmud (a book of Jewish civil and religious laws and ethical lore), it was the secret mystic word spoken by God when He created the world. The high priest then spits upon the cross, with obscene gestures and cries that are part of the sickening and blasphemous ritual that makes mockery of the ordinances of the church. These exercises are typical everywhere.

Occult bookstores are booming in almost every community. Spiritism, too, is on the increase. This term embraces a spectrum of practices from witchcraft to extrasensory-psychological exercises. Spiritists believe spirits can be called forth — through chanting, groaning, and prayer — to inhabit the bodies of the worshipers, to cure them of ailments, and to give them personal advice.

If people involved in such practices are not demon-possessed in the narrower and stricter definition of what that means, we would truly have to say that they are under a strong and mighty evil influence. Psychological explanations there may be, but one thing is certain: Satan is determined to take as many as possible with him toward his final defeat by the crucified and risen Christ.

What Does the Bible Have to Say?

For the individual who respects and believes the Scripture to be a reliable source of information, there is no doubt that demons exist in both the spiritual and physical world. They are pictured in the Bible as spiritual beings who seek to harm, influence, and possess persons who are in a state of alienation from God.

There are at least sixty-five references in the New Testament to demons. Only ten appear outside of the Gospels, and only once in the book of Acts (10:13ff.). This may suggest that Satan's forces were unleashed in an unusual manner when God was in a very special sense seeking to establish His sovereignty over the demonic forces through the death and resurrection of His Son Jesus Christ. There are very few sources alluding to demons in the Old Testament. But we do learn there that men worshiped them (Deuteronomy 32:17; 2 Chronicles 11:15, et al.).

Among the many references in the New Testament, there are several important points to remember. Demons did exist and they possessed certain people (Matthew 8:16; Mark 1:32, et al.). They were always subordinate to the power of Christ, who frequently cast them out of people (Mark 16:9; Luke 8:26-33, et al.).

It is significant to note that Jesus Himself believed in demons. This, in itself, should silence the critic who denies demon possession as a real phenomenon. Jesus was indeed a product of His time and culture, which recognized the reality of evil spirits. But He did not simply accept this view because His generation might have been hyper-superstitious. We cannot overlook the fact that He was the very essence of truth, for He said, "I am the way — and the truth and the life" (John 14:6). He could not be deceived by falsehood. These passages also describe some of the characteristics of demons and their behavior and we must consider them in order to better understand emotional abnormalities in people today.

Demon Possession and Mental Illness

Because the Bible states that demons do indeed inhabit men and affect their behavior, the legitimate question may be raised: Is mental disease demon possession? A brief evaluation of the biblical description of demon possession and the contrasts with mental illness will help to clear up the issue. It is true that demon-possessed people described in the Bible displayed certain strange behavior that sometimes characterizes people in mental wards, but it is also true that there are significant dissimilarities that should be carefully noted.

Many Christians have felt that people who have hallucinations give evidence of demon possession. Pastors sometimes are approached by well-meaning church members to pray for a loved one so that he may be cured of demon possession. But it is a gross oversimplification to equate hallucinations with demon possession. You may wonder how we can tell the difference.

Demons Are Allergic to Jesus

In the first place, it is possible in both conditions for the person to manifest bizarre behavior. Under both conditions, he may be fierce and manifest extraordinary strength. Violence may or may not be evident. However, in the case of demon possession as described in the New Testament, we note a certain peculiarity. A demon-possessed person always reacted strongly to Jesus and His disciples. " 'What do you want with us, Son of God?' they shouted. 'Have you come here to torture us before the appointed time?' " (Matthew 8:29). They wanted nothing to do with Christ.

On the other hand, people who are deeply disturbed mentally often are devoutly religious. Unlike the demons, they want to be close to Jesus or have some kind of a deep religious experience. The problem unfortunately, however, is that the religion of such a person may be hallucinatory, whereby reality itself becomes distorted to him and he imagines himself to be a millionaire, a great religious healer, Jesus, or Napoleon Bonaparte. In this condition, the hallucinatory vision or voice is a projection of one's own superego or conscience, whereas in demon possession, the Bible testifies to real and separate spirits, not projections of the person's sickness or fantasy.

We have never discovered that any person suffering with paranoid schizophrenia has been necessarily allergic to Jesus. The paranoid person is not suspicious of Jesus or Jesus people only; he is terribly frightened of everybody. He may believe that the whole world is out to get him if he is in a seriously regressed state. At this stage he may also become omnipotent himself and even become Jesus. He doesn't ask, as the demons did: "What do you want with us, Jesus?" He is Jesus. This is an important distinction to bear in mind.

Furthermore, nine out of every ten people we treat with this problem are already Christians; so they are not rejecting Jesus as did the demons mentioned in the Bible.

Frank is a perfect example. One day a Christian employer brought me one of his employees for treatment. He came to me because he heard that I was a Christian. He didn't want an ungodly psychologist because he felt sure that his employee was clearly demon-possessed. I met Frank and the employer the same afternoon. Frank started talking the moment he entered the office. He brought up everything, from the good old days to a bunch of abstract, nonsensical ideas and theories.

I was impressed with the fact that he seemed almost unaware that he was talking to me or anybody else. He was reminiscing from his own dream world. New ideas came to him so rapidly that he could not sort them out. He was confused, incoherent, and irrational. I learned by the use of direct questions, that he professed to be a Christian. He said he had accepted Christ about six months earlier and that he had a sincere desire now to be a better Christian. He mentioned that he started hearing voices at the time that he had broken up with his girl friend. He missed her so much. She was all he had and he couldn't bear living without her. In my further examination, it was apparent that he really was a Christian. He was concerned about living a better Christian life and he was attending a gospel-preaching church.

Typically, he had a tenuous touch with reality. His girl friend was the last tie that he had had with people. When this tie was broken, he pulled into his own world and began hallucinating. After a period of hospitalization and continued therapy, his relationships with people improved and the hallucinations disappeared. This took place over a period of several months.

This is the place to mention my theological conviction that no Christian can be demon-possessed. He may be influenced and harassed like everyone else, but not possessed. It is my view that the body of the believer is the temple of the Holy Spirit. When the Spirit of God indwells a person, that person cannot at the same time be possessed by the devil or a demon.

Many people have either been brought or have come voluntarily to our psychological Center, thinking that we could wave some kind of magic wand to help them find the Lord because they wanted to have their troubles disappear. Thus, they are actually seeking the Lord and are not allergic to Jesus as were the demons characterized in the Gospels.

Demons Are Separate Beings

The second important consideration in the biblical records show that the demons who possessed people were distinct and separate personalities. They were disembodied and always looked for a body in which to dwell. This is especially clear from one reference when Jesus cast demons out of a man from Gadarene. "The demons begged Jesus, 'If you drive us out, send us into the herd of pigs'" (Matthew 8:31). These disembodied spirits needed a body so desperately that they were even willing to enter the pigs of the field.

In contrast, the person with the psychotic hallucination condition emotionally withdraws from people. A demon wants to associate with people, whereas the psychotic has the opposite desire. The mentally ill person wants to withdraw so much that he progresses in fantasy until reality eventually disappears, at which point he creates his own internal world of reality.

Demons Are Rational

The fact that the demons mentioned in the Bible spoke in a rational manner is a third important distinction. They stated where they did and did not want to go. They communicated in a logical manner. They were like the devil who spoke clearly, with purpose and meaning, possessing the ability to carry on a very real dialogue. With schizophrenics, many times, we find their speech and logic very incoherent. We hear "word salads," and irrationalities that do not make any sense, in contrast to the speech behavior of the demons in the Bible. Jesus was able to converse with them in a way that does not suggest that demon-possessed people were mentally ill.

Demons Are Object-Related

Fourth, the narratives in the Gospels that depict Christ and the demons clearly show that for the demons there was a reality relationship. The demons had an ego identification — they knew themselves and they knew who Christ was. For this reason there was a literal two-way conversation and relationship going on.

In contradistinction, the people who are referred to us as supposedly being demon-possessed suffer from a loss of object reality, just as Frank did. The voices they hear are usually a schizophrenic hallucination. The hallucination is a person's attempt to relate once again to the external world from which he has drawn away. When we speak to people whose voices tell us definite things and we reply, then an external reality must exist outside of ourselves. But when the voices exist only within a person's mind and he thinks they are real, then we call him insane or say that this is a hallucination. The voices are manufactured by the person himself to find reality. We don't find this at all in the biblical descriptions of demon possession.

For Demon Possession — Sudden Cure!

Lastly, we note a marked contrast between true demon possession and a psychotic condition when we consider the cure for both. The Bible tells us the specific treatment needed in dealing with demon possession. "But this kind [of demon] does not go out except by prayer and fasting" (Matthew 17:21 margin). Christ claimed that demons were cast out only by spiritual means. Also note that in the cases where they were cast out it was a very sudden cure — the person was rid of the demon and that was the end of the problem. The mentally ill are not cured instantaneously when someone wills it.

Hallucinations are cured by psychological treatment, whereas demon possession can be cured only by prayer and fasting, as Christ indicated. Missionaries have testified of cases of demon possession in which the afflicted person's sensitivity and responsiveness to the spiritual have forced the demons to leave immediately.

We do not deny for one moment that demon possession exists today, especially in geographical areas where there is little or no Christian influence. There are enough reports from stable and emotionally well-adjusted missionaries to support the veracity of such phenomena.

But when it comes to a psychotic state, treatment requires a far different course of action and the cure in chronic illnesses is, ninety-nine times out of a hundred, of very long duration. The spiritual approach may serve the purpose of helping the person relate to God as an external being, but hallucinations clear up only when an individual's relationships with people improve and he is given a drug like thorazine to supplement the private therapy. If the person is able to develop a strong and stable relationship with his therapist, he may be helped considerably, but this takes time, in contrast to the sudden riddance of demons by people as shown in the Bible. The stronger this relationship becomes, the greater the relief from the plaguing symptoms. Once object relations are established realistically, the fantasy needs disappear.

This is something quite different from demon possession as described already. Every time a person with a psychosis has been able to locate the therapist in external reality and the relationship has been able to grow, the hallucination has disappeared. There is no praying specifically or fasting involved; it comes strictly by an improvement in relationships with people.

Each Situation Must Be Judged Carefully

The foregoing considerations have led me to the conclusion that people suffering from hallucinatory emotional illness are not demon-possessed, as some believe. Nor are the facts recorded in the Bible compatible with the view or theory that demon-possessed people were just bodily or mentally diseased.

I have never yet met a patient who would qualify from the biblical descriptions as being demon-possessed. In each case, after careful evaluation and diagnosis, we find these people to have a severe psychosis. Although deviant behavior may be explained by natural causes, this does not mean, of course, that people may not be demon-possessed.

It is extremely important for people who are untrained not to make sweeping generalizations based on hearsay or some isolated case. Each situation must be carefully examined in light of the Word of God and scientific diagnosis through testing and observation over a period of time. It is very easy for some Christians, especially those who like to dabble in the mysterious realm, to believe fanciful ideas about demons. But the responsible and caring person will bend every effort to consider all the evidence at his disposal before making a judgment.

15

Is Sin the Cause of Emotional Problems?

All Maladies Have Their Root Cause in Evil, but There is More Than One Method to Deal With the Effects of Sin.

THERE ARE THOSE who tell us that every emotional problem is the result of sin. Their thesis is "If you get right with God and confess every sin in your life, you will be healed from your emotional problems." Others say they have done this and have found it doesn't work. This should raise a question in our minds: Is healing emotional disorders as simple as confessing our sins or are there other possibilities? We have here a real problem, indeed, and it troubles many Christians.

We Must Test Reality

For us to say, in any sense of the word, that sin in the world is not real would be both a denial of reality and of the holy Scriptures. On the other hand, to say that a person's sin is the cause of all his emotional problems is, without question, not substantiated in reality. For instance, if a one-year-old child is disturbed so that he is not able to eat and thus withdraws, how can we conclude that this is only due to his having sinned? Again, how can it be sin when a person's terrible emotional condition, after it is examined over a period of time, is found to be the result of pressure on the brain or possibly even a tumor? Frequently, when the problem is treated medically, such a person will lead a normal life. Would it be fair to a person to say that his emotional disturbance due to such causes was the result of his sin?

Or, suppose a young child's mother dies. This little child is then left to seventeen different aunts and uncles who don't want the child but take it because they feel obligated. Could we say that any disturbance created by the child's not knowing who was his mother or father is a result of sin? We would be in grave error to answer yes.

I remember the time when some friends of ours brought their cute eight-year-old daughter to stay for a period of time at our home. Having three sons in my family has made me a little more responsive to little girls. I remember so well that she was the cutest little thing, with blond hair and blue eyes, just what I've always wanted in a daughter. When I saw her, I said, "Hi ya, Judy." I went toward her to throw my arms around her and she just froze and screamed. To her, it was just as if I were taking a knife and, with a vicious look in my eye, preparing to stab her.

A rain storm came and Judy had to stay a week longer than had been planned. Well, it took that whole week to thaw out that little girl. There was no question that she was emotionally disturbed. The men in her life had created many hurts. Her mother was divorced, and every man the daughter had been around was mean to her; so the thought of another man was a very frightening experience. Slowly, after I worked with her for a period of time, she thawed out and before the week was over she was very responsive to my affection.

Let's also consider the serious emotional problem of schizophrenia. There is much discussion today in the field about a component called "teraxein" in the blood of schizophrenics. Teraxein creates a certain chemical imbalance in their bodies. This is not found in other people. This being the case, we just can't say that their emotional illness is due to their own sin.

Many women who have lived a very normal life suffer various degrees of depression and emotional changes after having a hysterectomy. Are you going to say that every woman who experiences stress after a hysterectomy has these conflicts because of some sin in her life? That would not be a fair postulate at all. The same logic would apply to the menopause. A faulty endocrine gland and various estrogen imbalances also may cause a variety of emotional complications.

Emotional problems are closely related to mental retardation. Is retardation sin or is it not sin? There is a Bible passage that throws light on this issue. We have already dealt with the story of the child who was born blind. We pointed out that when asked who sinned, causing the malady, Jesus said neither the parents nor the child sinned (John 9:2, 3). The same analogy of sin would apply in the cases of retarded individuals.

A General Effect of Original Sin

There is another aspect of the issue of sin and mental illness that we must recognize. In another sense we would have to say that all maladies, maladjustments, physical diseases, and mental disorders are a result of evil. As evangelicals, who believe the Bible, we have to say that if there had never been the fall of Adam and Eve in the Garden of Eden, there would be no problem in the world. Before the fall of man Adam had no pneumonia or marital trouble. All was perfect bliss. There were no digestive blocks. We don't have any record in the Garden of Eden that anyone ever died of starvation. There were no social problems in that world. We have no record of guilt, fear, or any form of maladjustment. In fact, the picture we have of the Garden-of-Eden setting before the fall is similar to the biblical description of heaven. There was no corruption of any kind. After the fall of man, it is a different story. Man became fearful and guilty. Adam and Eve hid themselves from the presence of God. The record states that man would have to go out and work by the sweat of his brow because thistles and weeds and all kinds of irritants were going to become a part of his life. We would have to say, then, that all maladies of life — physical, emotional, and spiritual — really do stem from sin way back in the beginning and if man had never sinned, none of them would be present today.

This brings us back to our original question: Is emotional illness due to sin in one's life? Certainly, one would have to conclude that sin is the result of being born into a sinful world, but when we test reality, it is a tragic oversimplification to say that since all emotional and physical problems have their root cause in the sin committed in the Garden of Eden, all we have to do to cure these problems is to "plead the blood of Christ" and they will disappear. Practically, this, of course, is not the case. Paul testified to this in his letter to the Colossians in referring to Luke as "the beloved physician" (4:14). Paul did not reject Luke's profession. We wouldn't need any "beloved physician" if sin were the direct cause of all problems. All we would have to do would be to get right with God — then all the problems would disappear.

Again, why did Jesus say, "It is not the healthy who need a doctor, but the sick" (Luke 5:31), if doctors do not serve a useful role? As previously stated, certainly the physician of the mind or the "mind doctor" is just as valid as the medical doctor, especially when we realize that so many today are mentally ill.

Tragic Oversimplification

Many times the man of the world doesn't understand the Christian's simple message of salvation. They come to church and hear us say, "All you need is Jesus." This can be most misleading. Many go out, shaking their heads in a puzzled manner.

> One man in my office summed up this bewilderment when he said to me, "What a tragic oversimplification to hear the people say in a church service that all I need is Jesus. I walk out and say to myself, You mean we don't need food, clothing, or fellowship with other people? We don't need a family, a car, a home? It just doesn't make sense. My goodness me, according to them, all we need is Jesus."

We know that the statement about needing only Jesus is right, but
it can be wrongly understood. The idea needs to be qualified. Here
again we have one of the dichotomies in life. What do we mean as
Christians when we say, "All that I need is Jesus"? We should really
say, "All that we need for the salvation of our souls is the Lord Jesus
Christ. We need Him as the final and ultimate spiritual answer to
our existence. Also, we need Jesus to help us prepare and find ways
to meet the needs in life, such as clothing, people, family, car, etc. So
it is right to say that we do need Jesus; we need Him for salvation
and to provide the necessities of life, as well as for faith and wisdom
to guide us in the right channels."

But to oversimplify all of this to mean that Jesus is the answer for
absolutely everything in all areas of life is both dishonest and unreal.
It can give the world the wrong idea of what Jesus really intends to
do for us.

To this point it looks like we have presented a question and have
provided simple yes and no answers. On the one hand, sin is back of
all problems since the beginning of man, but on the other hand, its
effects are not simply handled with Bible verses. We're glad the Bible
refers to sin as the "mystery of iniquity." Much of life is like that and
there are paradoxes that complicate matters.

There Is Responsible Action

There is also a third area we must come to understand. We have to
recognize and accept the fact that sin can be the cause of emotional
problems. We don't deny that at all. What we object to is the view
that specific sin by the person is the direct cause of *all* of his emotional problems. Sin in certain situations may be a major contributing
factor. For instance, we may illustrate the result this way:

> I knew a man who in a fit of jealous temper, willfully slammed
> his fist through a pane of glass and got his hand slashed because
> he was in a very sinful state of anger. I say he reaped what he
> sowed. There are people who are emotionally driven to go out
> and do very foolish things.

The experience of the prodigal son in the Bible, who had everything
going for him in his father's house, is the classic lesson. We may
speculate that he had his own room, cattle, possessions, and a job.
One day his sinful pride led him to rationalize, *I'm sick and tired of
this life. I'm going to go out and live it up a little.* And so he said,
"Dad, give me all that belongs to me, so I can have a good time."

There was a willful rebellion in him and he went out to live as he
pleased. When he came to himself, tired of eating the husks that the
swine wouldn't eat, he returned to his father's house. If he had stayed
home, no doubt, he wouldn't have had some of the emotional traumas

that he did. So there are cases where emotional problems may be caused by deliberate, willful rebellion against God and His standards. But it would be a mistake to conclude that it is all caused by sin. There is a very fine line between sin and emotional causes of disorders. We must be very careful not to judge too harshly.

Missing the Mark

To better understand sin's true influence on us, we must take a look at the basic meaning of the term "sin." In the New Testament the Greek word is *hamartia*. We find the word used in the Bible 425 times. The root meaning of the word is "to fall short." It also means "to miss the mark," "to err," "to offend." We must conclude that, without question, sin is a biblical or theological term. It is anything that interferes with perfection or happiness. "Vice" is an ethical or moral term that defines evil that is against the right conduct of man. "Crime" is a legal term denoting any violation of a law of society. Now to say that when the secular man uses these terms, he is trying to explain away sin would be incorrect. Such terms are secular definitions of what the biblicist or theologian would call "sin." So the basic meaning of the word is missing the mark, falling short, erring, or offending.

The Levitical offerings in the Bible are very interesting. There is a difference between the sin offering and the trespass offering. The sin offering was to atone for the guilt of sin itself. The purpose of the trespass offering was not for the sin itself, but to repair the damage that sin had done. This distinction is very important. There is a great difference between the forgiveness of sin itself and dealing with the trauma or the effects that sin of the parent or the child has had on a person's life. This issue comes into sharp focus by the following illustration.

> I once heard a radio preacher say that men call alcoholics sick, but God calls them sinners and drunks. You could tell by the emphasis and glee in his voice that he lacked a basic understanding of their problems. I began to wonder, as I listened, if he really loved and cared about the people who have an alcoholic problem.

Of course, this same argument is presented to the psychologist. The common view of many people in the pew, as well as of those in the pulpit, is that the psychologist always explains away wrongdoing. Let's contrast these views and see if there is not something that will give us some further insight. Any way we look at the matter of sin, it is a very mysterious thing. How it works in both the conscious and the unconscious, how man's natural inclination is to believe a lie, how man has a tendency to take the road down rather than the road up are very real questions. Because we ask them, you can readily see that we're not trying to explain away sin at all. We recognize sin's existence and influence in all of our lives.

There Are Extenuating Circumstances

It would be valid, in clinical psychology, to suspect that a person who lives an immoral life and says he cannot control it has a weak ego. He doesn't have control of his impulses to stop acting out sexually. Certain theologians would come along and say, "Friend, this is nothing but pure sin, and you are trying to explain it away by calling it a weak ego."

Or the psychologist might say to a person who is filled with hatred, "This feeling is displaced frustration, and you are trying to get even with the world. By hating the world you are displaying the unresolved frustration and hostility that you have against your brother." Immediately, someone else comes along and says, "Wait a minute, you're trying to explain it away by saying that he had a frustrating experience in the past, and now he is not responsible for his act in the present. The Bible says that hate is pure sin."

Again, the underlying reason a child may lie is that he has a very sensitive disposition and temperament and he is fearful of being scolded. So in order to get by the anxiety that he can't handle, he becomes a persistent liar. By lying he doesn't have to deal with the anxiety. Once more, many Christians would say, "There you go again — you're trying to tell us that lying is not sin."

Take the case of the young man who cheats in school. Maybe the reason is that he is with a number of students who are very bright. He has an IQ of 91, and so in order to keep up his grade point with the rest of the class, he cheats on his exams. The psychologist may say that the boy feels very inferior about himself and he tries to compensate by cheating. Again, the typical reply would be that this is an attempt to excuse sin.

One final example — how about stealing or coveting? Two of the Ten Commandments deal with these sins. In therapy, a diagnosis may show that the person with this problem is one who never had anything as a child. He finds that he wants to go out and steal to get even with society. Or we occasionally find kleptomania in a woman who is a love-starved person trying to regain something she herself doesn't understand. She will steal because she is trying to get it back, whatever it is.

A person who covets is one who may have a deep inferiority complex and doesn't know how to go out and achieve material success like somebody else. In therapy we might find as we work with him on his unconscious level that we want him to gain a better concept of himself. And, as we do that, we can encourage him to go out and earn some of the things on his own. He then will feel better about having made it for himself. Then his need to covet other people's things will be greatly diminished.

These typical explanations are everyday occurrences in the psychologist's office and people who have these problems frequently respond very well to therapy. But immediately the theologian retorts, "But the Bible says that misconduct is sin and that is the only way you can interpret it because the Ten Commandments are very clear. Sin is sin — period!"

A Hopeless Contradiction?

All right, it appears on the surface that the theologian is saying that all abnormal behavior is sin, and it looks as though the psychologist is turning around and explaining everything by natural causes, thus repudiating the Bible. We cannot deny man's valid spiritual life and responsibility nor can we deny his psychological make-up and experiences, traumas, and problems in life.

What is the answer? As evangelicals, we want to be true to the Bible by not explaining away sin. It seems to me that the best answer in satisfying both the theological and psychological positions is this: Why should it be either one way or the other? Alluding again to the real meaning of the word "sin" in the original Greek, we feel that here is the key. Both positions cited actually fulfill the exact dimension and definition encompassed in this biblical term.

For instance, the person who has a weak ego and is given to temper outbursts obviously errs and "misses the mark" of maturity. Wouldn't we say the person who lies, for fear of scolding, "misses the mark" because he is not able to cope with it, take it on the chin, and rise above it? So, the psychological definitions are just as valid as the theological definitions in even the very meaning of the word "sin."

Jesus dealt with this beautifully as it is recorded in the Bible. We find Him integrating the ideas in a real sense. We can't overlook this. There is a story about Jesus helping the man who was sick from a palsy condition. Jewish scribes didn't like the idea when Jesus said to the man, "Your sins are forgiven." Seeing the viewers' anger, in essence Jesus said to them, "Well, what is easier for Me to say? 'Your sins are forgiven' or 'Take your mat and walk?'" (Mark 2:9).

What Jesus was really saying was that He wanted to draw men to Himself, no matter what the problem. He could save men in a theological sense from sin, or He could deal with their social or physical maladies, such as palsy in the above case, and raise them up. Both conditions are malignant conditions. Both conditions "miss the mark" of perfection. Jesus said in effect, "Take your pick, you can say it this way or you can say it that way. The important thing is that people are drawn to Me." Some individuals grow better with one type of exposure to life, others to another, and still other persons to several kinds — but when they are forgiven, they all mature and become more like Christ.

Two Sides of the Same Coin?

So then, can we not say that ultimately we are actually treating a sinful condition when we are treating an inferiority complex? Can we not conclude that we are really treating sin problems when we are helping a person get rid of his deep-seated hostilities toward his brother that are now converted into migraine headaches? Are we not dealing with the sin question when we help a person strengthen his ego and thus become more stable in his relationships with people? Treating injuries caused by "missing the mark" of perfection in this manner is as valid and real as in the theological sense.

On the other hand, if a man has not come to Christ, then we need to treat sin in the manner of a personal evangelist, leading him to Christ, using the message of the Bible. There is salvation in no one else. Then along with his growth in grace, we continue to make him mindful of Christ and his own sinful nature. Plus, we unclog the jets, help him face the hurts and the things that he can't face psychologically so that he can mature to the point where he lives a victorious Christian life.

This demands that we discern between good and evil when it comes to a method of treatment. We must treat all types of maladies with the particular kind of therapy that each needs. You remember it was stated earlier that every illness has a corresponding treatment. The same applies here. We need to be aware of whether the problem is spiritual or emotional or both. We must know when to support a depressed person and when to chisel away at the underlying causes. We must know when to be silent with a person filled with obsessions and when to speak. We must be ready to teach values and beliefs to one who has no value system and help one with poor values to change his point of view.

So, in helping a person overcome problems we also must assist in the growth of his sanctification as set forth in the Bible, for this helps the person to mature in his faith. Once again, we see that emotional and spiritual maturity are really two sides of the same coin.

Use the Proper Method

In my practice when a person comes and says, "I have a sin problem," I always take that at face value. I reply, "All right, how have you sinned?" I proceed to explain how he has sinned against God. Then I apply spiritual means to help him. If he says, "I feel separated from God; I'm not a Christian; I'm not saved," then my first goal is to use spiritual means to help that person. I seek to lead him to Christ. However, if someone says, "I'm all tied up inside; I go on sinning every day, but what good is it to confess again and again and again? What good is it going to do? I know I'm just going to do it again" — then I think we've got to get at the problem another way.

So instead of the matter being either/or, we can see that it really becomes a matter of immediate discernment as to what a person needs at a given moment. Jesus used various means in helping people. On one occasion He told a man to go wash in the pool of Siloam. Another time He recommended a different step and said, "Go show yourself to the priest." We may feel at times like saying, "You're really a sinner," but that may isolate the person. He might answer, "Yes, and you're the guy I can't talk to."

We must accept the fact that sin is with us and we need to deal with it in the best possible way at the moment. If the problem is not removed by the means of spiritual treatment of a patient, then we have to deal with the trauma that is caused by the sin nature and help the person through to become a fulfilled person.

For instance, consider a man who is an alcoholic. If we tell him he's bad and he goes home feeling so guilty about being bad that, in order to get rid of the guilt, he has to have another drink, we have accomplished nothing. By such an attitude don't we really isolate someone from the redemptive work of God? We need to think seriously about our approach to people.

For many people, when they hear the word "sin" from the pulpit, all they get is the feeling that they are bad. But really, the proper motive and incentive for going to church is to bring us closer to God because we realize that we are not bad in the theological sense but that we are in need of drawing closer to Christ because we "miss the mark" of His standard. This inspires and uplifts us to live a higher and fuller life for God and His honor.

One man said, "I just can't stand going to church anymore. After six days a week, with all the hassles at work, I need to be lifted up. All I hear every Sunday is how bad I am. I can't *take* going to church anymore." This is tragic.

The positive ministry of the church is to help us to assimilate the Word and apply it to our own lives in order to elevate us from a life of sin. How do we learn to relate it to life? How do we learn to apply it to our own personalities?

Room for Both

Therefore, we believe there is plenty of room for the ministry of the Word. There is also plenty of room for the psychologist. There is plenty of room for the person who deals with the social ills of mankind. In no way are we seeking to explain away sin. Where sin is the root problem, we need to recognize it and point the sinner to Christ.

Because of sin we must help to build people up in the faith, once they do receive Christ. Then a person finds that he can do everything through Christ, as Paul stated (Philippians 4:13). He can face his maladies and problems. Then he can say, "I can do all this through Christ who strengthens me."

But where other factors enter in to create emotional upheavals in a person, although they are caused indirectly by man's sinful nature, proper help by a psychologist or trained counselor will go a long way to help restore balance and bring adjustment and fulfillment.

16

Psychological Growth and the Christian Faith

The Bible Encourages Growth, but Growth Is Not Automatic

WHEN WE STUDY Christian maturity as revealed in the Word of God, we see many parallels with psychological growth. Since both the Bible and psychology deal with human beings — their nature, emotions, reactions, and development — this similarity seems quite natural. The Christian is, of course, adding a most important ingredient to his life — the spiritual. To understand and correct all the emotional problems in life seems incomplete unless there is purpose and meaning to the mysteries of life. The answers to man's existence are neither investigated nor solved by psychology alone, for the question of man's accountability to his Maker is not part of the content of psychology.

The ultimate answer to man's dilemma is in the "peace that passes all understanding," that is, his faith and reliance on God and his realization that grace is a gift of God freely given. Just as a watch would not exist without the creative genius of the watchmaker, man would not exist without the genuine hand of the divine Creator.

On the other hand, a man must have good judgment in his relationship with others. We have already explained that a good ego image is necessary before a man can have good relationships with others. Since no man has seen God at any time, it is possible for him to imagine God only in the parental role of his early childhood. If the man is halted in his emotional growth to a level we have described earlier, he might think God is doing things to him or saying things to him, whereas in reality they are nothing more than hangovers of parental discipline in childhood.

For example, if he learned from his parents that it is a sin to attend any other church than his own because they felt this particular denomination was the only one true to the Word, he may experience a sense of guilt when he attends a youth rally in a church of another denomination. He might say, "The Lord convinced me that I was becoming a liberal." In reality, however, it might be that the new church is as doctrinely sound as the one he attended all his life. He needs to learn that God is much bigger than any individual denomination and that His message can be heard by anyone who has ears to hear.

A man with good reality sense, then, can discern what is true, in spite of the crippling biases of past teaching.

What's Behind It All?

Earlier we referred to the man who believed that spiritual maturity comes only by reading the Bible, praying, attending church, and refraining from a select list of forbidden activities. Yet this same man can appear so immature, hostile, and hateful that we question his conversion or commitment. Is he harboring some unconfessed sin in his life?

Now, any of these things may be true, but if dealing with these spiritual areas of life fails to produce change, then we would conclude that to preach to him about sin and "getting right with God" will only increase his feeling of guilt and may even drive him away from the church and the Lord. As we pointed out in an earlier chapter, the problem is essentially spiritual; all man's trouble started with the fall of the first man, but the treatment of the problem demands more than spiritual worship and devotion.

The analogy of the physical disorder of appendicitis is helpful. This condition did not exist before the fall of man into sin or his alienation from God, because all was perfect. So we can reason that there would not be such a disease if sin had not entered the world. It would seem reasonable, then, that the disease is caused by sin. So, logically, if a man confessed all his sins, the appendicitis attack would disappear. But this is not the case, although James 5:15 states that "the prayer offered in faith will make the sick person well; the Lord will raise him up. If he has sinned, he will be forgiven." In chapter 15 we showed that the Bible also teaches that not *all* human ailments can be traced to sin in one's life, for John 9:2, 3 says, "His disciples asked him, 'Rabbi, who sinned, this man or his parents, that he was born blind?' 'Neither this man nor his parents sinned,' said Jesus, 'but this happened so that the work of God might be displayed in his life.'"

Since a man may suffer from different kinds of problems, it would seem right that we should try to determine the cause so that he may live a more victorious life for Christ. If a man has transgressed the laws of God by stealing, we expect that he would feel God's condemnation and hopefully sense the need to find forgiveness in the blood of Christ. However, if he suffers from a deep "free-floating guilt complex," which we discussed previously, he may confess to the Lord hourly and still feel no forgiveness. The problem is that he does not understand why he feels so guilty. Guilt is buried deep in his unconscious and manifests itself in such a way that even if the person knows his guilt is unfounded, he has no control over it.

A woman may come home after a day of sewing with a neighbor and find that she has a pair of scissors that belongs to the neighbor. She accidentally put them in her sewing bag. If she suffers severe guilt and anxiety and feels that she will be thought a thief, we may conclude that the incident triggered some deeper levels of guilt buried in the unconscious. The conflict is emotional and should be treated by psychotherapy. Perhaps she was accused of stealing as a small child, or perhaps she did steal and her mother punished her so severely that she experienced tremendous feelings of rejection. By reliving the old conflict that was not resolved in childhood and experiencing the conflict over again in a relationship to a new person with whom it can be resolved, the patient can experience a cure.

A Call for Action

The Lord desires for each of us personal growth and stability. If fulfillment and "wholeness" were not intended for this life, Jesus would not have said to His disciples, "Be perfect, therefore, as your heavenly Father is perfect." He was not upholding sinless perfection, for the word "perfect" means to be "fully grown," "mature," or "complete." Life does confront the believer with numerous tests and stresses, but a measure of attainment and victory is possible through the help of the Lord and by personality growth that enables us to cope with them. We are told in Hebrews 6:1, "Therefore let us leave the elementary teachings about Christ and go on to maturity." Maturity, here, is not to be thought of as "sinless perfection," but it means "Christian growth." We are also challenged in 2 Peter 3:18, to "grow in the grace and knowledge of our Lord and Savior Jesus Christ."

This process involves more than prayer and Bible study, for, as Joshua found, the Lord called for action. Joshua 7:10 commands, "Arise, why have you thus fallen on your face?" The Lord was admonishing Joshua that prayer has to be accompanied by action. Paul says in Philippians 2:12: "Work out your salvation with fear and trembling," and Luke says in Luke 13:24: "Make every effort to enter through the narrow door, because many, I tell you, will try to enter and will not be able to." Growth is not automatic. It is a process of accumulation of prayer, precepts, and principles incorporated into our daily life. The Bible gives us a long list of actions that reveal carnal and childish behavior that we are to eradicate in our growth toward grace.

It is interesting to note that the list of spiritually carnal traits is identical with what the psychologist calls "infantile behavior." In chapter four we discovered the stages of development in a child.

These same levels manifest themselves in adults who never "grow up." Christians who do not mature emotionally retain these early developmental characteristics, too. They are manifest in the way a Christian behaves in his relationship with other people. We cite a few of these parallelisms.

The Passive Christian

First, there is the *passive-dependent Christian,* who, like a small child, wants to have everything done for him. He is concerned because no one at the church ever calls on him. Of course, it would never occur to him to call on others. Then there is the passive Christian who feels that the church and the world should support him. He makes constant demands upon the "Deacon's Fund." He is always unemployed. The Bible says to him, "If a man will not work, he shall not eat" (2 Thessalonians 3:10). Another type of Christian feels chronically unloved. He is always looking for someone to love him. He has never learned that "it is more blessed to give than to receive" (Acts 20:35), and that in the giving of love he receives love in return (cf. Luke 6:38).

Christians with problems in this area may even have trouble with the constant need to incorporate something by mouth, such as gum, candy, pop, food, or even alcohol. Their appetites are uncontrollable.

The Bible teaches that men should move beyond this stage, "for the drunkard and the glutton will come to poverty, and drowsiness will clothe a man with rags" (Proverbs 23:21). This kind of Christian has never grown beyond the oral stage in his development. He may give money to the Lord's work, but his motives are manifest when he emphasizes his expectations of all the Lord will return to him. The part of Malachi 3:10 that he likes is the blessing he is going to receive from tithing, the open windows of heaven and the "overflowing blessing." His prayers abound with all that he wants God to give him. He is a "gimme" Christian.

The "Know-It-All" Christian

The second great area in psychological development is the *mastery stage.* Numerous illustrations of this type of behavior are found in the Scriptures. In Matthew 22:15 it is said that the Pharisees "went out and laid plans to trap him in his words." We see the argumentative Christian today who loves theological debate. He must always be right. We have described this kind of person in a previous chapter. When he discusses minor theological points, he feels that winning the argument or proving that the other person is wrong is much more important than finding the true meaning of God's Word.

He is constantly comparing. He is obsessed with right and wrong. He is a moral crusader. He may thank the Lord that he is not like other men as we see in the prayer of the Pharisee about the publican (Luke 18:9-14). He is the kind of person Jesus called a hypocrite — one of those who tithe "mint, dill and cummin," and "have neglected the more important matters of the law: justice, mercy and faithfulness," making "clean the outside of the cup and dish, but inside they are full of greed and self-indulgence" (Matthew 23:23, 25).

The hypocrite may be charming and hospitable in church or even a highly respected church official, but as soon as the door is closed at home, he is mean and cruel, punishing his wife and children. If his wife were to tell of her suffering to his friends at church, they wouldn't believe her. This man is similar to the Pharisees who have all their doctrines memorized and ceremonies mastered, but lack love, compassion, and concern.

The "Show-off" Christian

The third area of comparable psychological development is centered in *exhibitionism*. The Pharisees always put on a show, but Matthew 23:5-7 explains that "everything they do is done for men to see: They make their phylacteries wide and the tassels of their prayer shawls long; they love the place of honor at banquets and the most important seats in the synagogues; they love to be greeted in the marketplaces and to have men call them 'Rabbi.'"

We see the modern-day, counterpart Christian in many churches. If he can't direct the choir, he won't sing in it either. If he can't be one of the ruling elders, he may decide to attend a different church. Such Christians feel that their talents are not appreciated. They have to be the "big cheese." They are more concerned about their position in the church than the overall welfare of the church. They love compliments and are oversensitive to criticism.

The Growing Ego

All of these attributes are marks of the immature Christian. They are the childish things that the apostle Paul put away when he became a man (1 Corinthians 13:11). All these actions are illustrations of arrested ego development. The Lord uses testing and chastisement to strengthen the ego and to enable it to mature. For example, the Lord sent Nathan the prophet to King David to rebuke him with these words: "You are the man" (2 Samuel 12:7). Paul said in Romans 5:3, "Not only so, but we also rejoice in our sufferings, because we know that suffering produces perseverance." Perseverance, or patience, is an ego virtue. Learning to live with cantankerous people and learning to wait for the Lord in time of physical illness add to the strength of the ego. As physical exercise builds muscle tone and reduces fatty tissue, the ego, through experience, develops strength and tone. Instead of bursting forth with accusations against others, the Christian with a growing ego learns to control and understand his feelings and reactions. He is capable of insight into himself and others and, as a result, he is able to grow both in self-acceptance and spiritual grace.

This is the same condition that psychologists call maturity, because it is characterized by the ability to share with others one's self-worth as well as love for one's neighbor. Also, it is the realization that one is neither superior nor inferior to others. Thus, we see that Scripture and experience reveal the same laws for psychological growth.

It must be stressed that Christianity is not a crutch as many secularists suppose. It strengthens a person in four areas necessary to emotional maturity: (1) the capacity to love another person and become aware of his or her needs; (2) a sound, consistent conscience with well-formed moral precepts; (3) a sense of personal identity and of how others feel; and (4) the realization that one will die, and a way of coping with this prospect. When Christianity and the tools of psychology are both used, an individual has a more profound chance of reaching the *sumum bonum* ("highest good") of life here on earth.

In the next chapter we will deal in more depth concerning the function of therapy to assist in making psychological growth a reality.

17

Should a Christian Seek Psychological Help?

God Has Always Used People to Do His Work.
A Trained Counselor Is a Vital Link
for Rendering Needed Change.

HAVING ESTABLISHED in a previous chapter the right for psychology and therapy to exist, let us now turn our attention to a discussion of the purpose and role of therapy and a study of the biblical justification for psychotherapy, with a comparison of Christian views and psychotherapeutic concepts in the healing process.

A fully functioning person is one who is fully open to his own experience and can sense and interpret his immediate experiences without denial or distortion. Frequently, however, people by themselves are not able to perceive their world as it really is nor cope with everyday-life situations. The trained therapist may serve a vital role in restoring such people to lead healthy and fulfilled lives. Traumas and deep hurts in early life often create great anxiety, leaving the person with feelings of aggression, guilt, unworthiness, and depression. There may be hostility toward social sanctions, authority figures such as parents or the Bible, etc. Often these feelings may be turned toward the self and this will cause deeper problems.

A Key Supportive Role

The professional therapist, because of years of training, becomes the vital tool for rendering change in the individual. He guides and encourages the patient to do some work and to discover certain aspects of himself that had previously been too painful to accept. One of the great resistances to emotional growth and maturity is the fact that a person frequently has a "will to suffer" or a "will to be ill" in his neurotic pattern because he is afraid to face or cope with the underlying problem.

Thus the therapist does not always want to remove anxiety but prefers to get the person to face it, because the tendency is to push it down or postpone it. Sometimes the therapist will even create feelings of anxiety so the person will work to strengthen his ego and thus be better able to cope with harsh reality. The ego is lazy; so anxiety sometimes must be created to force people to see themselves as they are. The key role for the therapist is, of course, to be patient and empathetic, providing great support when the patient relives hurts and faces stresses.

This often means that a very deep relationship develops between the patient and the therapist because the feelings and expectations that the patient develops in the present situation are often memories and feelings that the patient actually lived through in the past and these are now strongly associated with the therapist.

Many Goals

The purpose and goals of therapy are varied. They may, in part, be summarized in the following manner:

1. To find why a person is afraid to develop emotionally, that is, if he is fixated at a traumatic point in life.

2. To help build and develop the ego so as to enable the individual himself to reconstitute his value system in conscious action.

3. To help the person reconstitute his defenses so that he can function better. This means trying to remove pathological defenses, making them more normal in terms of dealing with reality.

4. To help the person gain greater self-understanding through insight.

5. To help in creating an environment in which the person dares to face his feelings under more favorable circumstances.

6. To help the individual reorganize his own self-concept by integrating feeling, thinking, and action and so help him become a "whole" person, because only when the past is relived and the manifestations of it become clear to the individual by living through the trauma again will the patient finally be released from the anxiety or hostility that he has.

7. To induce free-flowing verbalization of problems so as to be able to get at the source of the trouble.

8. To help uncover in the person resistance that opposes self-knowledge.

9. To help bring into consciousness certain realities of which the individual is often unaware.

10. To help the patient lift the repressions or resolve them. Sometimes the same resistance or the same repressions will recur

again and again. They must be dealt with over and over before the person will finally abandon his old modes of thinking and neurotic patterns so that he may acquire a new life. Often the patient has the tendency to repeat his habitual defense patterns and forget what new insights he may have been given; so the person must repeatedly work through the same problems, releasing repressions until the new solutions are permanently remembered and the ego is strong enough to gain control to cope with anxiety in a normal manner.

Erich Fromm has summarized it well when he said that the purpose of therapy is to help the patient "gain" or "regain" his capacity for love.

In chapter 13 we touched briefly on the need for two-way communication — because we need each other. When we turn our attention to the Bible, we make an exciting discovery. It, too, enforces the need for the release of burdens and the dire need for believers to give of themselves to encourage and uplift those who are weighed down with severe problems.

People Need People

Moses said in Exodus 18:16, "When they have a dispute, they come to me, and I judge between a man and his neighbors, and I make them know the statutes of God and his decisions." Moses dealt with the personality problems among the people and then sought to reconcile them to God and His laws. In 1 Kings 3:16-28, Solomon judged the two harlots who wanted to claim the living son, and brought truth to bear on the question. Likewise, Priscilla and Aquila perfected the weak area in the eloquent Apollos' life through counseling with him. They "explained to him the way of God more adequately" (Acts 18:26).

Both emotional insights and spiritual insights come through the compassionate and delicate counseling of another human being. In Acts 8:30, 31, the eunuch read the Scriptures but did not have a deep awareness of what he was reading. Philip asked, "Do you understand what you are reading?" The eunuch replied, "How can I, unless someone explains it to me?"

James 5:16 says, "Confess your sins to each other and pray for each other so that you may be healed." There is healing and emotional release in talking to another human being. We cannot, however, be too careful in choosing the person in whom we want to confide. Again we are exhorted in Galatians 6:2, "Carry each other's burdens, and in this way you will fulfill the law of Christ." The process of spiritual maturity is also highly charged with the human element and personal counseling.

Walking with Christ means to follow His example and carry out His commands. Besides the verses on counseling and the carrying of one another's burdens, we find much ground for therapeutic help through studying Christ's life.

Jesus was always involved in three ministries: *teaching, preaching,* and *healing.* "Jesus went throughout Galilee, teaching in their synagogues, teaching the good news of the kingdom, and healing every disease and sickness among the people" (Matthew 4:23). The disciples were given the same commission (Matthew 10:1-8). Because we are the disciples of Christ, this is our commission, too. This means that we can be used of God to have a share in the emotional and spiritual ministries of healing.

The Greek word translated "heal" in these passages is the same word from which we get our English word "therapy," as was mentioned in a previous chapter. Therapy is the healing process of the mind.

Teaching is for the purpose of giving a knowledge of the truth.

Preaching is designed to touch the will, inspiring man to do something about the truth that he has learned.

Therapy, the healing process, enables man to sift through the good and bad human experiences until he is able to experience Christ as a stable object of faith unencumbered by emotional instability.

Professional Counseling Defines Identity

When a man expresses his faith, doubts, loves, and hates in the presence of the counselor, it helps him crystalize his own being, identity, and experience. In the presence of the counselor, he is able to experience the acceptance and love of Christ which he may never have had from his parents. It is in this new situation that he may experience the love of God. This therapeutic process is both taught and exemplified in the Word of God. "Praise be to the God and Father of our Lord Jesus Christ, the Father of compassion and the God of all comfort, who comforts us in all our troubles, so that we can comfort those in any trouble with the comfort we ourselves have received from God" (1 Corinthians 1:3, 4).

These verses establish forever the deep need we all have for our fellow human beings. Often when a person is in trouble, a well-meaning friend will say, "All you need is the Lord; just pray about it." But it is not enough to give out a set of laws and say to a person, "Now go do it." That friend does not recognize the fact that man is a social being and must relate to other human beings. Praying has its distinct purpose, but relating to others is one method God desires for the easing of burdens. Man is even better understood to be a social creature when we observe the mentally ill.

It's How You Look at Reality

In some psychoses, a person may think he is Godlike. He can do anything, buy anything, go anywhere at any time. He is God. He is supreme. He has taken his own ego as an object of self-love and is cut off from reality. This is why some psychotics seem to be so religious. Actually, when their experience is examined, their religion and concept of God equal self-worship. They become God, Napoleon Bonaparte, or Jesus Christ. It is definitely total investment in the self, sometimes described as megalomania.

Therefore, if a human being is to remain sane, he must always have good relationships with people or he will find himself in his own world of personal isolation. He first invests his emotional energy in mother, then gradually enlarges to father, siblings, peer group, spouse, children, grandchildren, and others.

Normal development means, then, that a person must constantly maintain a good relationship with other human beings in order to stave off the natural tendency of regression to the "omnipotent" position of the psychotic. He must give up himself as being autonomous and relate to reality as it truly is.

Since reality is always in a state of flux, he must continuously adjust to a changing reality. Loved ones live and die; so he must replace this love lost toward another person. He must also constantly invest love and psychic energy in objects (people and things) or he will lose perception of them. For instance, if a person never writes, calls, or visits his friends, they tend to lose importance to him and he begins to forget them.

This is why people need others and why man is a social creature. If a person is completely cut off from people physically or psychologically, he will experience emptiness, isolation, and even insanity. Man cannot survive by himself.

This is seen when we observe how a child learns. He learns abstract truth and love concerning God even at a very early age. He may believe and accept this truth and love, but it is necessary for him to experience love and acceptance from human beings to truly understand it. The process of spiritual growth is perpetuated through the human touch.

The Church of Christ needs ministers of counseling just as it needs pastors, teachers, and evangelists. Christian counselors who have been taught the love and comfort of God during their childhood can counsel the disturbed Christian and convince him of God's love, because they have experienced the love of God themselves and have the training to communicate acceptance and love to the disturbed person.

There Is a Place for Professional Help

Many Christians are critical of the person who feels he needs personal counseling. They feel he should simply rely on the Lord. This attitude only makes the emotionally disturbed person feel even more guilty about not yielding to Christ. This is an unfair criticism because we usually find that the person who solves his conflicts by spiritual means had a happy, secure childhood or was able to relate to another person in childhood outside of his parents in a loving, accepting way at the important junctures in his life. Having found comfort and acceptance through personal relationships, he is now able to relate to God without all the fear, doubt, and frustrations of childhood. This makes all the difference in the world.

The person who did not have these advantages will have his hurt feelings, guilt, and hostility buried so deeply in his unconscious that he has no idea of what is wrong. Nothing is more frustrating for a sincere saint of God than to be plagued by guilt and find no release in pleading for the blood of Christ to absolve his sin. Studies of human behavior reveal that the feeling of release comes only when the person is conscious of the *cause* of his guilt and is freed from it. Only the therapeutic process will bring the unconscious material into consciousness where the person can deal with it. Even after it becomes conscious, it may require a period of desensitizing and relearning so that he ceases to repeat the neurotic reactions and develops healthier responses to life situations.

The psychologist is a specialist in behavior and for this reason his knowledge is of use to a wide variety of people, groups, and organizations. But it must also be remembered that not everyone who seeks help from a psychologist has a severe emotional disorder. Many people have relatively minor or temporary difficulties or important decisions to make that can be aided by counseling in the relevant principles and facts of psychology. "Should I pursue a career in law?" "Why do I do poorly on exams when I know the material?" Minor marriage difficulties and problems in work, study, love, and life in general can often be helped with a little sophisticated psychological guidance. Clinical psychologists can counsel and guide in the problems of life as well as treat more serious emotional disorders.

Freedom in Christ

Another aspect related to our study is the analogy between the process of salvation for the sinner and the process of therapy for the neurotic. There is a striking similarity.

We shall look first at the plan of salvation. The Bible plainly teaches that when Adam and Eve ate of the forbidden fruit, fellowship with God was broken. Thereafter, all men were born into the world with a sinful nature. "In sin did my mother conceive me" (Psalm 51:5). All men then are aliens and foreigners, without hope and without God (Ephesians 2:12, 13). So Christ came into the world to pay the death penalty for man's sin. "The wages of sin is death" (Romans 6:23). Because all men are sinners, another sinner could not atone for man's sin. This required a pure sacrifice, a man without sin. Only Christ, the Son of God, was capable of bridging the gap. By the shedding of His blood He took upon Himself the sins of man. He paid the penalty for sin, therefore, "he himself is our peace" (Ephesians 2:14). The fellowship with God that was lost in the fall of the first Adam was restored in the Second Adam, Christ. The slavery to evil desire is now broken, and man is free. Note the emphasis on relationship in all these references. "So if the Son sets you free, you will be free indeed" (John 8:36).

In this life we are to grow in grace and the knowledge of Christ until His return when, "we shall be like him, for we shall see him as he is" (1 John 3:2). This sanctifying process is like love between two people. It is a joyous conflict of two self-conscious individuals who allow each other to remain individuals and who are ever working toward a final, yet never-completed unity. The unity between the believer and Christ is never complete until the believer reaches glory.

But What If I Can't Relate?

Now let us examine the process of psychotherapy. When a man comes for psychotherapy, he often feels lonely, estranged, and frightened. He is separated from people. He cannot understand how he can be among people, talk to them, work with them, and even live with them, and yet still feel empty and lonely. He is a stranger in the midst of people. He may talk to them, yet emotionally he has them shut out. He feels that if anybody really knew his thoughts, his feelings, and his desires, they would be shocked and reject him. He keeps everything bottled up; so he is tense and fearful of seeing himself for what he really is and afraid of what others think of him.

Therefore, when he comes to therapy, his defenses are up. He is frightened at the prospect of revealing himself. His hatred toward people may be covering up his fear of being hurt if he were to get too close to them. This feeling exists because he was hurt in earlier life by those close to him whom he trusted. His hostility may be a defense against seeing himself as weak. To be angry and tough may give him a feeble sense of being strong and untouchable.

Telling nice, tall tales during therapy may be his only defense against his feeling of inadequacy. He is like the little boy who feels inadequate in fighting the stranger, so he tells his opponent that his big brother will beat him up. He may lie about his grades in school in order to be able to fight off his feelings of intellectual failure.

Talking only about the present may be his way of defending himself against painful memories of the past that he has never dealt with. His desire to talk only of the past may be his defense against talking about something in the present that he doesn't want to face.

However, as he begins to talk, these defenses begin to break down. Inconsistencies show themselves and are pointed out to him without any condemnation. In short, the response from the therapist to this material is one of acceptance, understanding, and genuine concern. For the first time the patient feels accepted as a person and finds a friend with whom he can communicate. His feelings and thoughts begin to flow. As they do, new areas of resistance appear. He transfers onto the therapist many of the fears and doubts he once held toward his parents or other people. This response is studied and found to be unnecessary in the new relationship with the therapist.

Therapy Is Learning All Over Again

His old, neurotic, childish ways of responding are now relearned and fused into a more healthy mature response. As he continues to grow, he sees inconsistencies more and more within himself and connects them to surfacing repressed memories of the past. More and more the conflicts that have caused the headaches, depression, nightmares, and compulsions disappear. The conflict between the conscious mind and the unconscious has been resolved. His weak, staggering ego finds strength in the new healthy accepting relationship with the therapist. It is now safe to grow. He has completed an identification with the therapist that is healthy. Since the therapist accepts him, he can now accept himself. He feels like a new, whole person.

Because he has been shown love and acceptance by another person, he is now for the first time able to love others and himself. He can accept love and give it. Since he is emotionally no longer shutting people out, his sense of loneliness and estrangement disappears.

He sees people now in a *reality* context. Some are hostile and rejecting; so he sets up normal reality barriers against allowing them to hurt him. Others, however, are warm, accepting, and genuine. He can now develop lasting friendships, communicate, and acquire a sense of belonging.

Startling Parallels!

When we study and compare the processes of salvation and psychological therapy, we find much in common in man's search for a relationship with God and his search for relationships with people. In both, the individual finds himself cut off, separated, living precariously within himself, and anxious. In both, there is an agent that mediates to break through the wall. In the Christian faith,

Christ offers the sinner unconditional acceptance and grace. The sinner cannot earn it by his own merits; it is the gift of God (Ephesians 2:8, 9). He responds to it only by faith. Faith is the saving element. The man must believe in Christ with his heart and confess Him with his mouth (Romans 10:9, 10). The therapist, in order to help the patient, must be able to accept him as he is, too. It is this acceptance without condemnation that breaks through the wall of defense. The patient then develops "faith" in the therapist's abilities, understanding, and acceptance.

After personal salvation, there is growth in grace. There is communion with the Lord through prayer, Bible reading, and meditation. In therapy, too, after the initial walls are broken down, there is a growing, deepening relationship between the therapist and the patient. New maturity in the personality is developed, just as the Christian grows in his new-found faith.

Finally, as the Christian identifies more and more with Christ, he seeks to become more like Him and to heed His commands. He does this because he loves Christ. It is an impelling love and desire to maintain fellowship that cause him to live a Christian life — not back-breaking legalism. For instance, the teenager who gets into trouble with the law may develop an enjoyable relationship with the therapist. As a result of the satisfaction he receives from this relationship, the youth may be encouraged to give up his unlawful behavior rather than damage this relationship.

Does Therapy Work?

The question is frequently raised: "Does therapy work?" The development of psychological principles and application of them in the treatment of people, conclusively show that therapy does help numerous people. If a person is severely disturbed, psychology can "rescue" him to the point of bringing him back into reality so that he may more readily perceive his emotional and spiritual condition.

If a client has the ability to gain insight and wants to change, and if there is a warm relationship between him and his therapist, significant changes will take place. We have seen many people, even by a purely secular approach, overcome internal frustrations and anxieties so that conflicts are resolved. For these reasons secular psychologists as well as Christian counselors are capable of alleviating emotional disturbances in people.

Limited but Useful

Some secular psychotherapy has much value in it because it uses principles that are clearly found in the Word of God.

We cannot forget that unconditional acceptance of a person is offered only by God. His love and understanding for man is beyond our comprehension. And man can offer acceptance to another human being only on the basis of what man has been promised by God. Secular psychotherapy accepts man, too, but it ignores the theological aspects and makes an attempt to upgrade man's worth and productivity in this life. At best, then, it can never attain the lofty goals derived from the spiritual dimension because, as a secular field of knowledge, it leaves out man's accountability to God. It stresses self-reconciliation without taking into account much of biblical truth. Secular psychotherapy, then, is a "secular" salvation, but this does not mean that it is invalid or unimportant.

Secular psychotherapy also lacks another dimension found only in the spiritual. God is omnipotent; the therapist is capable of error. Secular therapy recognizes no eternal aspects, whereas the Christian believes in the reality of the unseen. God exists to him not just as a subjective experience or projection, but as true, objective reality. Only He can provide the basic inner tranquillity because He can forgive man his sin and give life beyond the grave.

But professional services for human beings, though limited, cannot be easily discredited. They may have great usefulness for the individual who cannot relate to people. It bears reemphasizing that before a person ever relates to God he relates to people (father, mother, etc.) in one way or another. And since a person is introduced to God through people, he may have to work through hang-ups with people in order to fully accept his peace with a loving God if those relationships were insufficient for a healthy personality development. This may require trained professional counselors who recognize the deeper dynamics of such a structure. God has always used people to do His work. The parent, the pastor, the missionary, the writer, and the trained counselor all are included in God's program to help fulfill all of man's physical, emotional, and spiritual needs.

The Pastor and Counseling

A discussion of this type would be lacking if some mention were not made of the significant role that pastors have in helping people. Their role is significant for especially two reasons. First, they have a great exposure in the community. The Joint Commission on Mental Illness and Health issued its final report for the United States Congress in 1961. It was a plea for more services to promote greater mental health in our nation. The report showed that the church is one key to enhance such a program because clergymen outnumber psychiatrists — at that time, thirty-five to one. Furthermore, for every person who went to either a psychologist or psychiatrist, more than two went to a pastor for help. Obviously, then, he has an important role in touching a large mass of people.

Second, perhaps more than any one person, the minister has the greatest opportunity to reach people who are hurting. The very term "pastor" implies that his function is more than that of a teacher. He should be close to his people and their problems because he has access to his parishioners' homes and his parishioners have access to him. People look to him as a model of a "good man" and to his home as an example of Christian family living; so they naturally look to him to help solve their problems. Therefore, he is able to perform some of the functions of a professional therapist.

Since counseling deals with the area of human behavior, some definite guidelines must be followed. Without certain skills and an awareness of the dynamics of human emotions, a minister can actually do more harm than good. Without adequate knowledge he cannot deal on a deep level with such things as loneliness, hostility, insecurity, depression, psychological guilt, rejection, and loss of self-esteem. He may lack certain skills because of a lack of training. More and more of our theological seminaries are including in their curricula required courses in counseling that involve knowledge of counseling techniques. This is a step in the right direction.

To get further training, the pastor should continue the educative process to acquire greater competence in this area. He should read available literature in the field and call in outside help to assist in family and personal life growth. He may also avail himself of the many programs offered in forms of seminars, workshops, etc., which will sharpen the tools for better counseling. There are schools and organizations that offer workshops on pastoral counseling.

Harm may also be rendered if the pastor has the common tendency without training to prejudge people or provide simplistic spiritual answers. Failure to refer at the proper time is another serious failing. The pastor should avoid playing with depth counseling where strong neurotic or psychotic patterns are evident.

Awareness of these problem areas will go a long way in overcoming some of these difficulties. Ministers will also be better counselors if they look inside themselves. Insight into the pastor's own emotional deficiencies will also serve as a means to be more effective, for he, too, is not above needing help for emotional growth and maturity.

The Problem of Suicide

The pastor's key role may be better seen if we discuss one important example of a concern with which he is often faced: the problem of suicide. The 1970s have been declared the decade of depression. The major cause of death among college students is commonly known to be suicide. With all the political scandals and sudden changes in value systems and all kinds of economic pressures, many a person has lost faith in society and is buckling under the pressure of all that is expected of him in today's world. Hotlines of numerous organizations receive hundreds of calls from desperate people stating that they want out.

Statistics tell us that 50 percent of all people who are emotionally distraught contact their clergymen first. What a wonderful opportunity this gives the clergy to be front-line soldiers in this plague that is very much with us today. It also forces one to face the grave responsibility which is placed on people in leadership to help in time of need.

When the minister is called on by a suicidally depressed person, he should bear in mind several things. From a psychological point of view, the suicidal patient may be telling him many things. On a simple level he may not be planning suicide at all, but may only be letting the pastor know how much he is hurting inside. It is a desperate cry for help. Other people may use it as a shock technique to gain attention. Others will use it as a form of manipulation whereby they can get someone to do what they want him to do. It may be phrased in this way by the girl who wants to keep her boyfriend: "If you leave me, I'm going to take my own life." Or the gaining of attention may be illustrated by the person who swallowed a bottle of pills and then immediately called a friend to brag about what he had done. Obviously, if he had really intended to take his life, he would have simply taken the pills and kept anyone from knowing about it.

Another kind of suicidal threat is fostered by a temporary loss of an important relationship with someone. When a person calls on the phone and says, "I'm going to take my life," he has probably just lost something or someone of significant value to him. He has been kicked out of the house; a dear friend has just been killed in an automobile accident; or he has just moved and is disillusioned with the job opportunities, the cost of living, or something else about the area that he does not like.

Causes Behind Suicide

Let us now consider some of the more serious forms of pathological depression so that the pastoral counselor may better recognize them.

1. *The desire to unite with a loved one who has passed on.* For instance, a widow may not have been able to adjust to her husband's death. The house is not the same. The loneliness is unbearable. The sense of emptiness is beyond imagination. She knows there is no way she can bring him back; so by taking her own life she feels that she will be able to join him where he is.

2. *The inability to cope with the pressures of adult responsibility.* Many people who have had their parents do everything for them —

their thinking, all their business arrangements, the paying of all the financial obligations — suddenly find themselves ill-equipped to make these important decisions of life. They experience what we call a state of helplessness. They have high aspirations but their ego growth is unable to live up to them all. This presents an impossible task and they, too, want out.

3. *Regression to an emotional period of infancy.* Psychology tells us that the state of the infant in the womb is by far the most perfect state of bliss within the realm of life. Since this leaves a memory trace within all human beings, the tendency is to regress emotionally to this period. Taking one's life seems to be the only equivalent to this state of bliss.

4. *Severe unresolved hatred toward a parent or other significant person.* It must always be borne in mind that a person who would take his own life is angry enough to take someone else's life, too. Because he feels terribly guilty for being angry at the loved one, it seems safer to turn the hostility upon himself. By killing himself he also kills them. It's like saying, "We'll both die together."

5. *Many suicidally depressed people have a severely deficient self-concept.* All feelings of self-worth are gone. They may have an obsessive masochistic fantasy as to how wicked, awful, and rotten they are. They end up with the delusional conclusion that "such a wicked person as I should be dead."

6. *Realization of illness and not wanting to be a burden.* Many people with malignancies, certain blood diseases, or crippling physical handicaps know in reality that they will never get better but only worse. They come to the conclusion, "Why should I be a burden physically and financially to my family? After all, there's no future for me. Therefore, I have a right to end my life now."

How the Pastor May Help

First, get the person talking about his feelings. A person who talks about his suicidal feelings is in less danger of acting them out than the person who quietly withdraws and will not share those feelings with anyone. As he talks these feelings out, he may even feel a new sense of relief. Because the counselor has been so kind in listening, things are not as bad as they once seemed.

Second, do not contradict the person's feelings. You can't talk a depressed person out of his depression. Avoid statements such as "John, things really aren't that bad." "Come on, snap out of it." "You really don't feel that bad." "I wouldn't let these things bother me." The depressive doesn't even hear what you say.

Third, be careful not to make the person feel guilty by telling him that he is harboring some sin in his life or that God is going to punish him if he attempts to take his life or that he is not going to heaven because he will have murdered and murderers will find their place in the lake of fire. Remember, his feeling of guilt is already driving him to suicide. People like this feel exhausted, weak, and guilty and need to vent their hostile feelings within the range of an accepting ear. If they are open to spiritual advice and counseling, it is so important to show them passages in the Bible which build them up — passages relating to God's love, His concern, His ability to help in hours of testing and that He will see them through this time of crisis.

Fourth, work out with him any reality problems that may be available by showing him new ways of coping. Maybe the person sees only one solution to a given problem. "If I can't have her, then I know no one else would want me." For instance, to make a statement like this at age twenty-one, when the person is handsome and talented but misguided, would be by far too narrow a conclusion. He would do well to learn to reach out into new groups and meet other new people, and he may find, much to his surprise, that there are many girls who would wish to date him. To the person who has had a sudden break in a relationship we must offer ourselves to become the bridge towards building a new and better level of relating to other people.

Fifth, if the problem is not caused by any precipitating reality event, it may be what the psychologist calls endopsychic. In other words, it is caused by a deep internal conflict of which the person is unaware. It is unconscious. In this case it may be important to refer the person for professional help. If nothing is found after a physical examination, a clinical psychologist should be brought into the picture to make the deep, unconscious conflict conscious so that the person will be able to resolve it.

Sixth, an acutely suicidal person must always be watched carefully and in most cases should be hospitalized until he can work through the areas in his life that have precipitated the crisis. It should also be borne in mind that acute problems are usually much easier to treat because of their recent onset and because there is no long past history of similar difficulties. Chronic problems of long standing, on the other hand, often date back to conflicts in early childhood and may need long-time psychotherapy and possibly continual medication.

Some General Guidelines

Many fine books are available to pastoral counselors. Clinebell suggests nine things to be followed in ministering to the needy:

1. Listen intensively.
2. Use questions carefully to focus on conflict areas rapidly.

3. Help the person review the total problem. This tends to produce a clearer perspective and prepare the person to make an enlightened decision. It also helps him to mobilize his inner resources.
4. Provide useful information.
5. Focus on the major conflict, problem, or area of decision with the aim of clarifying viable alternatives.
6. Help the person decide on the "next step" and then take it.
7. Provide guidance when it seems useful.
8. Give the person emotional support and inspiration.
9. Move into longer-term counseling if brief counseling does not prove adequate.[1]

What Are the Differences?

Many people wonder about the difference between the psychologist and the psychiatrist. The clinical psychologist has an academic degree (Ph.D.) rather than a medical one (M.D.). He usually has more extensive training in psychology. The two primary activities of the clinical psychologist are diagnosis and treatment of emotional problems. These may be as specific as a "reading deficiency" or as general as a "neurosis." By using information from tests, interviews, and observations, the clinical psychologist attempts to diagnose the exact nature of the patient's difficulty.

The psychiatrist, being a medical doctor, prescribes drugs and administers shock treatments, whereas a clinical psychologist does not. He also diagnoses and treats emotional disorders. His emphasis is usually more medication-oriented. He usually gears his work to a shorter period of time, most often because of the higher fees he charges. Quite often, especially in hospitals, the clinical psychologist and psychiatrist work as a team.

Another type of practitioner frequently mentioned is the psychoanalyst. His title comes from a particular theory of personality therapy he employs — psychoanalysis. He may be a Ph.D. or an M.D., but his specialized training is in psychoanalysis.

A More Vital Function

The Christian psychologist has all the more a vital function to fulfill in helping people face their deep internal conflicts. Clinically, he is a psychologist. There is no specific school of Christian psychology. The difference is that he is a dedicated Christian practicing psychology and will therefore govern his clinical interpretations and

[1] Howard J. Clinebell, Jr., *Basic Types of Pastoral Counseling* (Nashville: Abingdon Press, 1969), pp. 88-92.

guidance according to Christian principles. He can truly help people to cope with conflicts in terms of human as well as spiritual relationships because he has both the secular and spiritual worlds at his disposal. This gives him a decided advantage. He can truly administer to the whole person.

In the next chapter we will discuss the greatest therapist of all — Jesus Christ, the "Great Physician," who, in the midst of a counseling situation, blended together the emotional and spiritual sides of man in a most revealing manner.

18

Christ and Hurt People

A Lesson on Counseling Procedures From the Life of Christ

A CLOSE INVESTIGATION of the biblical material about Christ will disclose the great amount of time He spent in counseling and in personal involvement with people and their problems. Christ is a perfect example of good counseling. Although He emphasized doctrine and spiritual values, He had much concern for people and their tribulations. He was neither aloof nor compromising. He ate with publicans and sinners. He never developed a sense of false human superiority. He was approachable, and people were drawn to Him. He never condoned sin, but He always accepted the sinner as a person and tried to raise him to a higher and holier life with God.

In this chapter we want to show how Christ, the Master Therapist, did His counseling and used perfect techniques to reach a disturbed person, thus encouraging emotional and spiritual growth.

A passage that illustrates this is John 4:1-30. This is commonly referred to as "Jesus and the Woman at the Well." As the story begins, we find that though Jesus was divine, He was also totally human, for He was weary from His journey and rested by Jacob's well at Sychar. In approaching the woman, He found the most common meeting ground possible. All the residents of the area came to get their water at this well. Christ appealed to the most common of all physical needs, the need for water, by saying to her, "Will you give me a drink?" He knew that there must be some point in common if two people are to communicate. He directly involved her by making a request that forced her to reply. Communication began. She asked Him questions and He replied.

He let her talk and she began to reveal herself, with all her fears and biases. She said, in essence, "You are a Jew and I am a Samaritan; don't you know that it is customary that we have no communication? We are rivals. Are you aware that I am a Samaritan and that Jews hate us because we have sold them into slavery? We have even killed Jewish pilgrims who were going to Jerusalem to worship. We have lighted false lights to throw off the regular beacon fires that Jews use to announce the beginning of months."

She implied that He was making a mistake, since Jews don't have dealings with Samaritans. This response, however, in no way threatened the Savior. He didn't react with horror or deny the Samaritan prejudice against Jews.

By His calm demeanor He indicated to her that He knew all the time that she was a Samaritan, but He accepted her as a person instead of being bound by convention, custom, or prejudice. She experienced shock and found herself needing to respond to Him simply as a person. Suddenly she learned that not all Jews were alike.

Encouragement

At this point Christ encouraged and drew her out even more by appealing to her sense of curiosity. "Jesus answered her, 'If you knew the gift of God and who it is that asks you for a drink, you would have asked him and he would have given you living water'" (John 4:10).

He was implying that He had some answers to life that she did not have. He knew she was looking for a deep and abiding relationship with a person with whom she could identify. We know this to be true because she had had so many husbands. Jesus offered Himself in a new and permanent relationship, indicating that He could give eternal life. Just as water satisfies the deepest longing of physical thirst, so Christ wanted to meet the deepest longing of her spiritual and emotional thirst.

It is at this point that our Lord faced the problem of communicating on the woman's level. She was still dealing too much with conscious reality — water — while Christ was trying to deal with her on a much deeper symbolic level of spirituality. It was much like the conflict that the apostle Peter experienced when he said he would never deny his Lord, yet he did so before the rooster crowed three times. He also was unaware of the deeper level of his own consciousness.

The woman asked Christ how He could give living water when He didn't even have a rope with which to draw up the well water Then she began to entertain some thoughts that led her in the right direction. She wondered if this man could be greater than Jacob and if He had great insights about life in areas that she couldn't understand.

Now that she had begun to deal with things beneath the surface, Jesus commenced to tell her why she was blind and could not see. He explained that the water — the level of existence on which she was living — always left her needing more, while the water He was talking about — the *living water* — would spring up to eternal life. He told

her it could be found through Him and would satisfy the deeper need
in her heart. He advised her to forget all her traditions about the
greatness of Jacob and past teachings and to enter into a relationship
with Him. He explained that He was interested in treating the *source*
of her problem and not the *symptoms.*

At this point she was motivated to trust Him. Empathy and trust
had been established, for she said, "Sir, give me this water so that
I won't get thirsty and have to keep coming here to draw water."

A Word for the Counselor

When a relationship had been created, Christ tactfully touched the
sensitive spot in her life, or the root of her problem, by saying, "Go,
call your husband and come back." She was suddenly compelled to
face herself regarding the total inadequacy and failure of her life. A
fulfilled life begins with the realization and acceptance of what we
really are.

The facade that she had so carefully guarded, the part of her life
she had never wished to discuss, was suddenly brought into the open.
She either had to defend herself against it by telling a lie or face it
with all the fears of being rejected, unloved, or condemned. Her
decision was made with caution. She would tell the truth, but omit
the details. She said, "I have no husband." Jesus faced her with the
whole truth, saying, "You have had five husbands, and the man you
now have is not your husband."

The dark area was now revealed. But the interesting thing in
Christ's counseling is that He then commended her twice for telling
the truth. Some people feel that when misconduct or evidence of a
sinful life is revealed, it is a compromise not to brand it immediately
and condemn the person. Just because the counselor accepts the
person doesn't necessarily mean that he condones his behavior. Unless
the disturbed person feels accepted, the counselor loses his chance to
understand and help. As stated previously, many people's sinful
activity is motivated by severe emotional conflict that drives them to
do things they otherwise would never do. Treatment is best achieved
by developing a relationship with the patient who, because of acceptance from another human being, finds enough strength to face his
deeper conflicts and give up the neurotic pattern of acting out his
anxiety.

This is the type of counseling Jesus engaged in here. He accepted
the woman for herself and commended her for her honesty without
condemnation. Because of this acceptance, religious biases and beliefs
that had kept her from a true communication and vital relationship
with Christ began to surface.

She started defending the traditions of her religious fathers about places of worship. Jesus promptly contradicted these traditions and said, "You have to get your eyes off doctrines, places of worship, and tradition. The day is coming when nobody will worship in this mountain or in Jerusalem. You don't even know what you are worshiping. You are lost in names and geographical locations and have forgotten that the true end of all faith is found in a relationship with God. Since God is a Spirit and can be reached only by faith, it is here you will find the meaning to life and the living water I have spoken of." Suddenly, in Christ's counseling process, far different levels of communication began to merge.

One of the laws of psychological interpretation is not to provide any diagnostic interpretation to the patient until the therapist feels that the patient is ready to accept the interpretation. Notice how beautifully the woman's and Jesus' thinking — separated by tradition, race, and religion — suddenly blended. The woman discovered the Savior without His revealing His identity. She said, "I know that Messiah (called Christ) is coming. When he comes, he will explain everything to us" (John 4:25). She wondered if this man was the Christ, the one who would lead people into a right relationship with God. Now that she was ready to accept it, Christ did not hesitate. He revealed Himself by saying, "I who speak to you am he."

This woman was then liberated from her neurotic world of self-isolation and self-containment for the first time in her life. She was captivated with Christ. The flow of love toward an object outside of herself completely changed her world, her life, her philosophy, her motivation, her morals, and her faith. Literally, all things became new!

The proof of these changes can perhaps best be illustrated by what we suggest may have been going through the woman's mind when she left her waterpot to contact the men in the city. From this action we can see the evidence for her conversion to Christ. Perhaps she left the waterpot because her life was so captivated by a new affection that she just forgot it. Maybe she was so anxious to tell others about what she had found that the pot would be added weight and might slow her down in getting to the city. Perhaps she realized that material things were now secondary to her new-found relationship. She had literally tasted of His living water and had lost the yearning for regular water. Possibly she wanted to leave her most valuable possession at His feet as evidence of her love for Him. Or she might have left the waterpot as a guarantee that she would return and bring the men from the city.

How much we can learn from Christ's counseling: making the correct approach to building a relationship, involving the other person, and understanding his biases and doubts!

We see the noncondemning spirit as the motivating force that leads people to a higher and better life.

A Word for Every Christian

Christ shows us in this story that perhaps the most important thing we ever do is to relate to people in a meaningful way and to help them.

All too frequently, our churches today have come through with a very harsh view of people. On principle, our evangelical churches should be the most loving and forgiving because they are the very ones who understand the Cross the best. Therefore, we need today more than ever what Dr. Bernard Ramm calls "redemptive ethics." This means that we are concerned not only about the eternal salvation of an individual but also about saving a whole life now or picking up a person at the point of tragedy and from that point on trying to redeem that life.

If we don't really understand this redemptive love, then we will come across only as hurting people. In our self-righteousness, we separate them from the church. Redemptive ethics says, "Yes, your life is a mess up to this point; it is tragic. But from here on out, let's make the most out of it that we can. This isn't the end of life. In God's grace let's make the very best out of the picture."

There are many people who are truly hurting. Christians are often quick to write others off. But if we really want to be like Christ, we must see hurt people as miserable, despondent, and extremely unhappy. They are often very lonely people who are desperate because of emotional scars left by divorce, alcoholism, immorality, etc. We can't tell these people to cop out on life because they have failed, or make them feel as though they are second-class citizens.

Extend Real Forgiveness

We must come to them with a redemptive spirit, holding out to them the possibilities of a mended life, starting now. Even though their self-image is demolished, we may offer hope. They are hurting for understanding and acceptance. Therefore we must have an ability to practice real forgiveness and not be judgmental or purely moralistic.

So being redemptive means that there will be acceptance, and acceptance means that we will be realistic, for anyone can get himself into a situation that may become almost unbearable.

The heart of our Lord is better summarized in the context of love, rather than in the law of "an eye for an eye, a tooth for a tooth," a law which He reinterpreted and strengthened. He was not morally soft, but reached out in love to people, thus helping rather than hindering them.

This book will have served its purpose if through it you are brought to a point of greater sensitivity to people who need to be healed from maladies of the body, mind, and spirit. Then, together, we will be fulfilling the imperative of God's Word: "Carry each other's burdens" (Gal. 6:2).

Become a Whole Person

Thus, we see Christ's tremendous power of blending the psychological and spiritual together, first by eliciting personal involvement with Himself as a human being followed by a personal relationship with Himself as God. Again, we want to stress that man is not whole unless the physical is cared for. Also, man is not whole unless he is willing to deal with his emotional problems and relate to others. And, finally, man is not whole until he is one in a relationship with his Maker — a relationship that is possible only through a relationship with Jesus Christ, God's Son.

When the physical, emotional, and spiritual are blended together in their right and proper places, man becomes whole and can courageously face that future day when all secrets will be revealed and he will be one with his Maker, forevermore.

Bibliography

(RECOMMENDED READING)

Psychology of Religion

Drakeford, John W. *Psychology in Search of a Soul.* Nashville, Tennessee: Broadman Press, 1964.

Ferm, Robert O. *The Psychology of Christian Conversion.* Old Tappan, New Jersey: Fleming H. Revell, 1959.

Fromm, Erich. *Psychoanalysis and Religion.* New Haven: Yale University Press, 1950.

Klausner, Samuel Z. *Psychiatry and Religion.* The Free Press of Glencoe, 1964.

Maslow, Abraham H. *Religions, Values and Peak Experiences.* New York: The Viking Press, 1964.

Norborg, Sverre. *Varieties of Christian Experience.* Minneapolis: Augsburg Publishing House, 1937.

Roberts, David E. *Psychotherapy and a Christian View of Man.* New York: Charles Scribner & Sons, 1950.

What, Then, Is Man? A symposium of theology, psychology and psychiatry. St. Louis, Missouri: Concordia Publishing House, 1958.

Sociology of Religion

Ellul, Jacques. *The Meaning of the City.* Grand Rapids, Michigan: William B. Eerdmans Publishing Company, 1970.

Reich, Charles A. *The Greening of America.* Bantam Books, 1971.

Schaeffer, Francis A. *The New Super Spirituality.* Downer's Grove, Illinois: Inter-Varsity Press, 1972.

Yinger, J. Milton. *Religion, Society and the Individual.* New York: The Macmillan Company, 1957.

Zuck, Roy B., and Getz, Gene A. *Christian Youth: An In-Depth Study.* Chicago: Moody Press, 1968.

Important Books in Psychology

Bruno, Frank J. *The Story of Psychology*. New York: Holt, Rinehart, & Winston, 1972.

Fitts, William H. *The Experience of Psychotherapy*. New York: D. Van Nostrand Co., Inc., 1965.

Fordham, Frieda. *An Introduction to Jung's Psychology*. New York: Penguin Books, 1953.

Frankel, Viktor E. *Man's Search for Meaning*. New York: Pocket Books, 1959.

Freud, Sigmund. *Psychopathology of Everyday Life*. New York: A Mentor Book, 1951.

————. *Totem and Taboo*. New York: W. W. Norton & Co., 1950.

Harris, Sidney J. *The Authentic Person*. Niles, Illinois: Argus Communications, 1972

Jourard, Sidney M. *Personal Adjustment*. New York: The Macmillan Company, 1958.

Maltz, Maxwell. *The Magic Power of Self-Image Psychology*. New York: Pocket Books, 1964.

Stone, Irving. *The Passions of the Mind*. New York: Signet Book from New American Library, 1971.

Tarachow, Sidney. *An Introduction to Psychotherapy*. New York: International Universities Press, Inc., 1963.

Psychology in the Church

Frame, John D. *Personality*. Chicago: Moody Press, 1961.

Oates, Wayne E. *When Religion Gets Sick*. Philadelphia: The Westminster Press, 1970.

Powell, John S. J. *Why Am I Afraid to Love?* West Los Angeles: Argus Publishers Corp., 1967.

————. *Why Am I Afraid to Tell You Who I Am?* Oakland, California: Peacock Books, 1969.

Whitlock, Glenn E. *Preventive Psychology in the Church*. Philadelphia: The Westminster Press, n.d.

Counseling

Clinebell, Howard J. *Basic Types of Pastoral Counseling*. Nashville: Abingdon Press, 1966.

Morris, J. Kenneth. *Marriage Counseling: A Manual for Ministers*. Englewood Cliffs, New Jersey: Prentice-Hall, Inc., 1965.

Oates, Wayne, and Lester, Andrew D. *Pastoral Care in Crucial Human Situations*. Valley Forge: Judson Press, 1969.

Oates, Wayne E. *The Bible and Pastoral Care*. Grand Rapids, Michigan: Baker Book House, 1953.

Family Relationships

Briggs, Dorothy. *Your Child & Self Esteem*. Garden City, New York: Doubleday, 1971.

Drakeford, John W. *Games Husbands and Wives Play*. Nashville, Tennessee: Broadman Press, 1970.

Duvall, Evelyn Millis. *Why Wait Till Marriage*. New York: Association Press, 1965.

Ginott, Haim G. *Between Parent and Teenager*. New York: Avon Books, 1969.

Miles, Herbert. *Sexual Happiness in Marriage*. Grand Rapids, Michigan: Zondervan Publishing House, 1967.

————. *Sexual Understanding Before Marriage*. Grand Rapids, Michigan: Zondervan Publishing House, 1971.

Mundey, Carol. *The Divorced Mother*. New York: McGraw Hill, n.d.

Osborne, Cecil. *The Art of Understanding Your Mate*. Grand Rapids, Michigan: Zondervan Publishing House, 1970.

Small, Dwight H. *After You've Said I Do*. Old Tappan, New Jersey: Fleming H. Revell, 1968.

————. *Design for Christian Marriage*. Old Tappan, New Jersey: Fleming H. Revell, n.d.

Wright, Norman. *Christian Marriage and Family Relationships*. Glendale, California: Church Press, 1972.

Important Books by Christian Psychologists

Collins, Gary R. *The Christian Psychology of Paul Tournier*. Grand Rapids, Michigan: Baker Book House, 1973.

Darling, Harold W. *Man in Triumph*. Grand Rapids, Michigan: Zondervan Publishing House, 1969.

Dolby, James R. *I, Too, Am Man*. Waco, Texas: Word Books, 1969.

Hyder, O. Quentin. *The Christian Handbook of Psychiatry*. Old Tappan, New Jersey: Fleming H. Revell, 1971.

Knight, James A. *A Psychiatrist Looks at Religion and Health*. Nashville, Tennessee: Abingdon Press, 1964.

Larson, Bruce. *No Longer Strangers*. Waco, Texas: Word Books, 1971.

Mavis, W. Curry. *The Psychology of Christian Experience*. Grand Rapids, Michigan: Zondervan Publishing House, 1963.

Oates, Wayne E. *Religious Factors in Mental Illness*. New York: Association Press, 1955.

_____. *What Psychology Says About Religion*. New York: Association Press, 1958.

Tournier, Paul. *Guilt and Grace*. New York: Harper and Row, 1962.

_____. *The Meaning of Persons*. New York: Harper and Row, 1957.

Walker, Harold Blake. *To Conquer Loneliness*. New York: Harper and Row, 1966.

Index